Building for a Long Future

The University of Chicago and Its Donors, 1889-1930

By Brandon L. Johnson

with Daniel Meyer, John W. Boyer, and Alice Schreyer

The University of Chicago Library 2001

4,000 copies of this publication were published in conjunction with an exhibition held in the Department of Special Collections, University of Chicago Library, May 2 through December 31, 2001.

The University of Chicago Library Society provided support for this publication.

©2001 University of Chicago
All rights reserved. For permission to quote or reproduce from this catalogue contact:
The University of Chicago Library
1100 East 57th Street, Chicago, Illinois 60637
www.lib.uchicago.edu/e/spcl/

Design and typesetting by Lynn Martin.
Production editor Valarie Brocato.
Printed by Universal Press, Niles, Illinois.

Cover and page 9 illustration:
Emery B. Jackson, Harper Memorial Library, Architect's Midway Perspective, Study 1, 1915. Archival Photographic Files.

Page 11 illustration:
Burton-Judson Courts, plaster cast model of the University of Chicago Coat of Arms, December 18, 1930. Archival Photographic Files.

ISBN: 0-943056-28-4

If in any small measure the work of my life can contribute to the advancement of knowledge and the greater happiness of men; if this can be done in the city where my busy days have been spent and where my heart is; and if, as I believe, we, who have aided in the work of erecting this great University, have helped to lay the foundations of what can never be destroyed, I feel in this work a pride and happiness that have never been equalled in my life.

SIDNEY ALBERT KENT TO WILLIAM RAINEY HARPER

Note read at the Fifth Convocation
1 January 1894

Table of Contents

Preface 7

Introduction 9

Founding Donors 14
    George C. Walker
    Martin A. Ryerson
    Creating Women's Residence Halls
    Buildings for Teaching and the Arts
    Helen Culver
    John D. Rockefeller

Enhancing the Campus 26
    Annie McClure Hitchcock
    Anita McCormick Blaine
    Harper Memorial Library
    LaVerne Noyes
    Julius Rosenwald

Supporting Research and Learning 36
    Scholarships, Fellowships, Lectureships, and Prizes
    Howard Taylor Ricketts
    Jesse L. and Susan Colver Rosenberger
    Frank W. Gunsaulus
    Enriching the University Library

Expanding University Resources 46
    The University Campaign of 1924-26
    Shirley Farr
    Harold H. Swift and the Swift Family
    Frank R. and Frances Crane Lillie

Culmination of an Era 56
    Developing the Medical Center
    Institutional Donors
    Max Epstein

Preface

On June 5, 1889, seventy delegates from local Baptist churches assembled in the Grand Pacific Hotel on LaSalle Street in the heart of Chicago's financial district. They had been summoned into urgent session by the Chicago Baptist Ministers' Conference and Chicago Baptist Social Union. Just three weeks earlier, at a dramatic denominational meeting in Boston, American Baptists had learned of John D. Rockefeller's pledge in support of a new institution of higher education in Chicago. In a letter dated May 15, 1889, the wealthiest Baptist in America had stated that he would contribute $600,000 toward the first one million dollars in endowment "for a college to be established at Chicago," but only if a sum of $400,000 in additional funds was pledged by other donors before June 1, 1890.

Spurred by civic pride and denominational loyalty, the delegates at the Grand Pacific Hotel embraced Rockefeller's challenge and launched a campaign to raise the needed funds. Once denominational sources had been exhausted and the campaign was still short of its goal, Thomas W. Goodspeed and Frederick T. Gates, the University's two principal fundraisers, turned to the non-Baptist business leaders of Chicago for support. Their appeal was answered with a generosity few could have anticipated. The $400,000 goal was met and exceeded, and in the process the University acquired a new set of influential backers—commodity traders, publishers, bankers, manufacturers, and merchants—who would form the core of its support in the years to come.

Today, Rockefeller's challenge pledge of 1889 and the munificent gifts he made in the years that followed are recognized as one of the most important departures in American private charitable giving. In throwing his lot with the new institution, Rockefeller confirmed the financial prospects of the Chicago venture and initiated a pattern for his own personal philanthropy that was to have far-reaching impact on areas of modern society as diverse as education, agriculture, civil rights, medicine, science, and international affairs. For their part, the trustees of the University of Chicago never doubted the crucial nature of Rockefeller's support, and in November 1892 they voted unanimously that the words "Founded by John D. Rockefeller" be added to all the University's printed material and be inscribed on the University Seal.

Less frequently remembered is the equally bold generosity of the other supporters who joined Rockefeller in establishing the University. Drawn from many different backgrounds and representing diverse fields of achievement, these early donors to the University, many from Chicago and an impressive number of them women, helped shape a distinct and vigorous tradition of giving. Their wealth, like the city of Chicago itself, was new, little of it older than the first or second generation. Their interest in the University was immediate and personal, not based on social convention or lengthy school ties of family and tradition. Their gifts were often of substantial size, especially for an urban leadership that was also being called to support the creation of libraries, academies, museums, theaters, hospitals, and charitable institutions of all kinds. And their philanthropy was remarkably farsighted, both in its quick grasp of fleeting opportunities and in its discerning anticipation of the next generation's needs.

This exhibition provides a fresh appraisal of these motives and achievements by examining a representative group of donors to the University of Chicago during its first forty years. While the exhibition highlights some of Chicago's wealthiest and most powerful philanthropists, the group also includes a number of donors of more modest means whose gifts to the University supported essential academic programs, scholarships, and research collections. Small or large, the gifts described in this exhibition should be seen as only one segment of a much broader array of donations of all types that enhanced the University in its early decades and continued to benefit the University for more than a century.

In focusing on early donors and their gifts, the exhibition is also able to do little more than suggest the crucial role played by University presidents, administrators, and faculty members in developing relationships with supporters and shaping the buildings and programs that realized their hopes. William Rainey Harper, the University's first president, was unrivaled in his devotion to the promise of higher education and his ability to draw support to the cause of the University of Chicago. The University owed much to Harper's persuasive skills, which were as evident in the office of tycoon Charles T. Yerkes as they were at the lectern before the Chicago Woman's Club. Faculty members such as educator John Dewey, physicist Albert A. Michelson, sociologist W. I. Thomas, and archaeologist James Henry Breasted were each adept in different ways at finding receptive donors and presenting their research needs in compelling terms. And Ernest DeWitt Burton, a faculty member who later became president, exemplified the ideal of an academic leader who was able to harness educational dreams to the goals and schedules of a demanding capital campaign.

Finally, a word should be said about the comparative size of the gifts mentioned in the exhibition relative to today's inflated dollar. The Consumer Price Index maintained by the U.S. Bureau of Labor Statistics since 1913 provides one standard of comparison for the purchasing power of the dollar over the past nine decades. Using the Consumer Price Index, a gift of $1,000 in 1913 can be calculated to be equivalent to more than $17,700 in today's economy. A gift of $200,000 would be worth the equivalent of more than $3.5 million. And John D. Rockefeller's cumulative gifts of $35 million to the University of Chicago from 1889 to 1910 would be worth no less than $620 million today.

Building for a Long Future: The University of Chicago and Its Donors, 1889-1930 is based on correspondence, minutes, photographs, architectural plans, and other historical records of the University of Chicago Archives in the Department of Special Collections. Additional materials for the exhibition are drawn from the Manuscript Collections and Rare Book Collections in the Department of Special Collections and the General Collection of the University of Chicago Library. Unless otherwise noted, materials reproduced as illustrations in this catalogue are from the University Archives.

The exhibition was undertaken at the initiative of John W. Boyer, Dean of the College of the University of Chicago and Martin A. Ryerson Distinguished Service Professor in the Department of History and the College. Dean Boyer played a central role in shaping the themes of the exhibition and contributed substantially to refining its emphases. Brandon L. Johnson, doctoral candidate in the Department of History, conducted the archival research and wrote the basic text for the exhibition and catalogue. Alice Schreyer, Curator of Special Collections, made important additional contributions to the research and writing.

The design and installation of the exhibition and the production of this catalogue were the responsibility of Valarie Brocato, Exhibition and Preservation Manager in Special Collections. Lynn Martin designed the catalogue, and the results testify to her practiced eye and elegant style.

DANIEL MEYER
Associate Curator of Special Collections and University Archivist

Introduction

In his 1916 history of the University of Chicago's first quarter century, longtime Secretary of the Board of Trustees Thomas Wakefield Goodspeed accorded an esteemed status to its early donors. They resolutely stood by the institution, he wrote, as it "passed through periods of extraordinary difficulty and no small peril." While the University's shortcomings "tried [their] patience and tested [their] loyalty," he wrote, they still "carried it triumphantly through all its difficulties." The University's benefactors "became in very many instances its fast friends and were always ready when the need arose to repeat their gifts," often more than once. Generous donors almost single-handedly brought the University of Chicago, as he put it, "out 'into a wide place,' with its future assured."

Goodspeed's chronicle, like most other institutional histories, lacks a truly critical perspective and occasionally rises to hyperbole. Not all donors to the University were so stalwart that they remained forever loyal to the cause. The institution had its reluctant patrons, its offended benefactors, and its soured contributors. But Goodspeed was correct in arguing that it enjoyed many extremely generous champions. By 1930, a growing number of Chicagoans, as well as alumni and other contributors from outside the city, had given the University millions of dollars to create a beautiful campus and support distinguished research and teaching programs. In a very real sense, these individuals created, funded, and maintained the University of Chicago.

These founding donors did not, however, invent the idea of a university in Chicago. As early as the middle of the nineteenth century, Chicago had been the site for another institution of higher education named for the city, one that was profoundly different from the university that eventually succeeded it in name and mission. The first discussions about a university in Chicago were responses to an announcement by Senator Stephen A. Douglas in 1856 that he would donate a section of land on the city's near South Side to the religious denomination that would build a college on it. The Presbyterians considered Douglas's offer but chose to decline. So a group of local Baptists, led by First Baptist Church pastor John C. Burroughs, mobilized themselves and secured title to the land. The organizers then selected a board of trustees, including Senator Douglas as its president, and in January 1857, by act of the state legislature, the college was incorporated as the University of Chicago.

A Baptist institution from the start, the Old University of Chicago (as it was later legally renamed) relied heavily on local congregations for support. A few wealthy Baptist benefactors put up some of the money needed for initial building construction and other needs, but subscription drives among interested Baptist congregations provided most of the cash for operating costs. This method kept the college solvent in the short term, but in order to remain afloat the Trustees decided to borrow money using the University property and building as collateral. Over time, the college began to plunge into greater debt, each liability slowly squeezing more life from it, until the insurance company holding the mortgage foreclosed on the loan. In 1886, the first University of Chicago was finally forced to close its doors.

Yet within two years, members of the newly formed American Baptist Education Society (ABES) and several leading citizens of Chicago started thinking about rebuilding. Although most members of the Chicago civic and economic elite in the 1860s and 1870s had provided little support to the first university, the decade of the 1880s saw the emergence of a younger generation with great private wealth. Baptist and non-Baptist civic leaders alike were persuaded that Chicago vitally needed its own major institution of higher learning. Forming a diverse coalition of religious and business leaders, and energized by a pledge from Baptist oil tycoon John D. Rockefeller, these Chicagoans joined a campaign to create a new University of Chicago and thereby to establish the city of Chicago as a proud home of one of the great universities in the world.

Accompanied by his fellow Baptist clergyman Frederick T. Gates of the ABES, Rev. Thomas Goodspeed undertook hundreds of personal solicitations during 1889 and 1890, meeting with many of the city's social and economic leaders and seeking the $400,000 necessary to match the initial pledge of $600,000 made by Rockefeller in May 1889. Such work was time consuming and often very frustrating. But persistence and perspicacity paid off, and Goodspeed and Gates were able to recruit a body of willing benefactors for the new University. The new institution opened its doors on Saturday, October 1, 1892, when students, faculty, and administrators crowded into Cobb Hall's first-floor chapel room to launch their first academic year with hymns and prayers.

Given the lofty scholarly ambitions of the new University and President William Rainey Harper's willingness to reach out to members of all religious groups, the institution quickly demonstrated a wider appeal than its predecessor and attracted the support of a broader circle of donors. True, devout Baptists had initiated and led the university effort, and it was owing to their sponsorship that Chicago received Rockefeller's initial support in the first place. But the idea of Baptist predominance, while still paramount for some of the faithful, did not inspire most of the major donors who supported the second University. New contributors from among the city's non-Baptist civic leaders were less interested in advancing any confessional cause than they were taken with the idea of raising their city's cultural prestige. While a majority of the University's Trustees were required to be Baptists, most of the institution's major donors came from much more diverse (often non-Protestant) religious traditions. Staunch and lapsed Baptists joined Catholics, freethinkers, members of the Jewish community, and religious independents in responding to the University's needs.

In fact, it is difficult to define a typical donor to the new University of Chicago. Few contributors possessed all of the qualities that late nineteenth-century American philanthropists are often supposed to represent: white, male, Anglo-Saxon, and Protestant, while also occupying elite social positions and holding politically conservative ideological views. Many donors were sufficiently wealthy to have their names attached to buildings on campus (such as Blaine, Walker, Cobb, and Swift), but numerous financial contributions were made by less influential or less wealthy Chicagoans. Likewise, and of possibly greater significance, the generosity of male donors was easily and quickly matched by a series of munificent gifts by women. Without the generosity of Chicago's women philanthropists, many University residence halls, scientific laboratories, and educational training programs would never have been established.

What actually motivated people to give to the University? Many scholars have suggested that the University's patrons, like major contributors to other Chicago cultural institutions, thought of their philanthropy as a way to lift the lower middle and middle classes to greater cultural sophistication and social stability. Also, if Chicago was to be the major metropolis and capital of the American West, it surely needed first-rate museums, libraries, and universities. And a surprising number of wealthy Chicagoans felt themselves responsible for building and maintaining these institutions. For many of these wealthy philanthropists, a rich (and prosperous) urban cultural life promised social peace and a virtuous, middle-class citizenry. Initially missing from such formulations, however, was a desire to address the educational needs of larger, working-class audiences. Some scholars claim that it was not until after the turn of the century, with the Progressive emphasis on the rationalization of public life, that the benefactors of Chicago's cultural institutions actually came to address these issues.

A close look at the donors included in this exhibit bears out these conclusions about Chicago philanthropy. Early contributors to the University had numerous motivations for their philanthropy. Some gave in order to memorialize associates or loved ones. Others gave because of their pride in their city. Some may have given to advance political and religious causes. And once Progressive ideas about the need to improve public life were expressed in the patterns of philanthropy of wealthy Chicagoans, donors to the University of Chicago also began to target their contributions toward easing the inequities of class and gender, both on campus and in the city at large. Such an extraordinary diversity of motives is itself central to the fascinating early history of the University of Chicago.

In his eulogy for University Trustee Charles L. Hutchinson, who played so critical a role in the founding of the University, President Ernest DeWitt Burton observed in 1924 that "through personal association with him in this work, I learned how accurate was his judgment, how inexhaustible his patience. He had a keen sense of the influence of architecture on the formation of taste, and a strong desire, happily shared by many of his associates, that what the University built should be so built that it would stand and be worthy to last. He built for a long future."

The same could be said for all of the women and men who are represented in this exhibition. The University of Chicago's remarkable and distinctive success in the world of higher education over the past century cannot be understood without recognizing the daring and vision of an extraordinary group of resolute donors whose generosity continues to sustain the University they made possible.

11

I have watched with growing interest the progress of the institution, the care of which has been entrusted to you. I am persuaded that there is no more important public enterprise than the University of Chicago. It seems to me to deserve the most liberal support of our citizens.

Silas B. Cobb

Letter to the University of Chicago Board of Trustees, 9 June 1892

Founding Donors

George C. Walker

In the late 1880s, the first University of Chicago had hardly gone into bankruptcy when advocates of a new university, led by Thomas Goodspeed, began scouting for land in the Chicago area on which to build their campus. A location within the city itself was an obvious choice, but an offer of property in the suburb of Morgan Park from real estate developer George C. Walker (1835-1905) complicated their decision. A onetime trustee of the Old University, Walker offered the Baptists a thirty-acre site near the Baptist Union Theological Seminary at 111th Street and Hoyne Avenue, along with a building that was already standing on the property and twenty-five thousand dollars. Walker, as the developer, naturally expected to gain from the agreement, since the University's construction would likely attract more residents and businesses to Morgan Park. As it turned out, his proposal was declined in favor of a site donated by Marshall Field on Chicago's South Side in the newly annexed township of Hyde Park; but Walker's continued enthusiasm for the new institution earned him appointment as a member of the first Board of Trustees, positioning him to become one of the University's major early donors.

Walker's relationship to the second University of Chicago grew out of a longer family tradition of support for denominational education. Beginning with his father Charles, who garnered influence as a noteworthy businessman and two-time president of the Chicago Board of Trade, Walker and his family readily answered the call to help establish a Baptist college—the first University of Chicago—in the city. His father was even tapped as a Trustee and served as Vice President of the Old University's Board until his death in 1869. George then agreed to take his father's empty seat, despite the fact that he found the rationale for denominational education less persuasive than had his father. As a young man George Walker was educated at institutions with strong religious values—Chicago's Temple Academy, Beloit College, and Brown University—but a dispute with a congregational disciplinary committee in Chicago over dancing caused him to sever his ties with the city's Baptist establishment. Neither Goodspeed or Harper seem to have viewed Walker's break with his religious roots as a liability, however, and once elected to the Board of Trustees in 1890, he remained an active and thoughtful member until his death in 1905.

In fact, Walker flourished as a Trustee and worked extremely hard for the University. He used family connections to help secure Silas Cobb's pledge in 1892 to fund construction of the University's first classroom building (Cobb was the father-in-law of Walker's brother William), and he also convinced his good friend and fellow businessman Sidney Kent to give $235,000 to construct a new chemistry building. He then demonstrated his own support in June 1892 by promising $130,000 to finance the building of a geology museum and laboratory on campus. Completed in 1893, the Walker Museum was a source of anxiety for the Trustee-donor soon after its opening. Due to a lack of classroom and office space elsewhere on campus, several other academic departments had been moved into the building. As Walker saw it, having departments take up space in the museum interfered with the building's original mission, which was to advance knowledge of the geological sciences. "The housing of other departments has crowded out the original intention of a building," he complained to his fellow

George C. Walker, n.d.
Archival Photographic Files

WALKER MUSEUM.

Walker Museum, Henry Ives Cobb, architect, architectural drawing, n.d. Archival Photographic Files

Walker Museum, exhibition area, n.d. Archival Photographic Files

Trustees in 1902. He implored his colleagues to return the museum to its rightful purpose by making "suitable appropriations" in the budget "so that now the work can go forward as originally planned, and so that I can see more of the good results in my lifetime." After several years of strenuous lobbying, he eventually persuaded President Harper to restore Walker Museum to its intended scientific function.

Martin A. Ryerson

Like his fellow capitalist George Walker, Martin A. Ryerson (1856-1932) also had long-standing personal connections to the city. His father Martin had moved to Chicago in 1851, where he soon made a fortune in the lumber trade, supplemented by shrewd investments in Chicago real estate, local banks, and the Elgin Watch Company. The younger Ryerson was to become one of the most important civic leaders in the first half century of the University's history, not only because of his extraordinary generosity as a donor, but also because of his distinguished leadership as President of the Board of Trustees from 1892 until 1922. Ryerson's initial appointment to the Board in 1890 proved to be a shrewd political move on the part of the new University's administrative leaders. Ryerson's lack of Baptist affiliation made him the perfect person to attract other non-Baptists to the cause, while his ability to command the respect of Chicago's elite gave him the personal credentials to serve as a key spokesman for the University.

Supported by his good friend and fellow Trustee Charles L. Hutchinson, Ryerson as President of the Board dealt admirably with an array of perplexing challenges, including the constant annual budget deficits run up by President William Rainey Harper. Calm, unflappable, patrician in his bearing, and having an unusually refined level of aesthetic sensibility, Ryerson easily reconciled his dual roles as administrative leader and major donor, while playing a decisive role in the planning of the campus and in defending its remarkable architectural unity and integrity.

Ryerson was educated in a fashion befitting his father's wealth, attending private schools in Paris and Geneva and graduating from Harvard Law School in 1878. After his father's unexpected death in 1887, when he was thirty-four, Ryerson became his father's sole heir and was free to devote much of his time to the establishment of the University of Chicago. Indeed, by the early 1890s, Ryerson retired from active business altogether in order to dedicate himself fully to his various philanthropic interests and his passion for art collecting. Martin Ryerson also shared his administrative talents and fortune with several of Chicago's other noteworthy cultural institutions. A trustee of the Art Institute of Chicago since 1890, Ryerson's knowledge of art was on the level of a connoisseur, and upon his death in 1932 the Art Institute was bequeathed a breathtaking

Martin A. Ryerson, n.d.
Gift of Mrs. C. Philip Miller.
Archival Photographic Files

Martin A. Ryerson to
William R. Harper, cablegram,
June 13, 1892. University
Presidents' Papers, 1889-1925

collection of French Impressionists—including five paintings by Renoir and sixteen paintings by Monet—and an extraordinary group of Old Master paintings as well, all of which originally hung in the Ryerson mansion at 4851 South Drexel Boulevard. In 1894 Ryerson was also appointed Vice President of the Field Columbian Museum, where he succeeded in rescuing a number of exhibits left after the World's Columbian Exposition closed in 1892.

Ryerson's financial gifts to the University were extensions of his work as a University Trustee and his life as a cultural philanthropist. Perhaps his most significant gift was $350,000 toward the construction and subsequent renovation of the Ryerson Physical Laboratory. He also played a key role in creating the new University's Library, for Ryerson was the primary figure in President Harper's successful campaign to acquire the Berlin Collection in 1891, providing almost half of the money that was secured to purchase the collection. Overnight this collection transformed the University's fledgling library into a major research collection, giving Chicago the second largest university library collection in the United States by 1896. Ryerson's interest in rare books and manuscripts found continued expression in his support for the acquisition of the famous Sir Nicholas Bacon Collection of early English manuscripts in 1924 and his funding of the purchase of a mid-fifteenth-century codex (the "McCormick Manuscript") of Chaucer's *Canterbury Tales* in 1930, both acquired on the basis of personal interventions with Ryerson by Professor John Matthews Manly of the Department of English.

When John D. Rockefeller offered a major pledge in 1906 to build the Harper Memorial Library, Ryerson also promised $25,000 to the same cause. To these gifts Ryerson added a major endowment to create the Martin A. Ryerson Distinguished Service Professorship in 1925. At the time of his death in 1932, Martin A. Ryerson's total contributions to the University of Chicago exceeded $2 million, not including part of a $6-million-dollar bequest that was evenly divided among the Art Institute, the Field Museum of Natural History, and the University of Chicago.

Ryerson Physical Laboratory,
from south, n.d.
Archival Photographic Files

Beecher Hall, student room, photograph by Capes Photo, 1935. Archival Photographic Files

Elizabeth G. Kelly, n.d. Archival Photographic Files

Creating Women's Residence Halls

One of the University's most pressing obligations in its first years was to provide adequate housing for its students. A successful college experience, President Harper believed, required adequate on-campus living quarters, although University officials conceded that they were not in a position to provide every student with housing. Residential opportunities for women students were particularly problematic, since plans for women's residence halls were still incomplete even after the University opened its doors in 1892. Rooms in boarding houses and apartments scattered around Hyde Park served as a temporary solution to the housing problem. In addition, administrators in 1893 temporarily reassigned female students to Snell Hall, a men's residence hall funded by a $60,000 gift from Henrietta Snell. Yet officials knew that relocating students to different locations on the campus was only a short-term solution and that sufficient housing would have to be built quickly to respond to the needs of the University's women students.

Deans of Women Alice Freeman Palmer and Marion Talbot made forceful cases to compel the University to provide suitable residences for women. Under their leadership and with the support of other University administrators, especially William Rainey Harper, major donors for women's housing were soon identified. Elizabeth Kelly, among the most important of them, had been married twice—first to Carlo Hull of Lower Sandusky, Ohio, and then Hiram Kelly of Sacramento, California. When Hiram died in 1889, he left Elizabeth a considerable fortune, which she used to support philanthropies including the University of Chicago. Elizabeth Kelly not only gave $62,000 dollars to build Kelly Hall in 1893, she also contributed an additional $70,000 six years later for Green Hall, named in honor of her parents. In a final act of great generosity, Kelly left $150,000 in her will to build the Classics Building, designated the "Hiram Kelly Memorial," which was completed in 1915.

Other donors readily matched Kelly's enthusiasm. The same year that Kelly Hall was built, Mary Beecher and Nancy S. Foster each gave $50,000 to build two additional residence halls. Beecher Hall (named after the donor's late husband, Jerome) cost only a few thousand dollars more than the amount originally budgeted. Foster Hall, however, was both larger and more expensive than Kelly, Green, and Beecher Halls immediately to its north. Nancy Foster was born to a Scots-Irish family from New Hampshire and came to Chicago in 1840 as the wife of Dr. John H. Foster; she took up residence with her daughter after her husband's death in 1874. A Unitarian for

17

much of her life, Foster could have distanced herself from the early Baptist orientation of the University of Chicago, but she gave to the University freely without any direct solicitation. After the initial planning for Foster Hall was finished, University officials found that the building could not be erected for the amount donated. On instructions from Nancy Foster, however, her daughter assured the Board of Trustees that if the University built the residence hall, the family would pay the entire construction cost. Moreover, when the University decided to enlarge the building in 1900, Nancy Foster again agreed to pay the costs of expansion. In all, she gave more than $83,000 toward the building. Because of ill health, Foster was able to see the completed building only once before her death in 1901.

Buildings for Teaching and the Arts

The new University of Chicago was fortunate in assembling a host of major donors much more rapidly than its predecessor. The Trustees of the Old University had raised slightly more than $100,000 to launch the construction of their rather modest campus at 35th Street and Cottage Grove Avenue in 1857, but these funds were hardly sufficient to cover the full building costs or ongoing operating expenses.

The financial situation enjoyed by the second University was very different. The safety net created by John D. Rockefeller's largesse, always given with careful deliberation, was both supportive and prescriptive, supportive in the sense that his gifts underwrote current academic operations and provided for long-term endowment, but prescriptive because Rockefeller insisted that his money should not be used to erect buildings. This strategy compelled University leaders to find other donors—such as Silas Cobb, Adolphus Clay Bartlett, and Leon Mandel—who were willing to pay for the costs of building construction.

Silas Cobb's gift, which was used for the construction of the University's first building, was especially significant, not only because it provided a centrally located building on the early Quad-

Silas B. Cobb, n.d.
Archival Photographic Files

Snell Hall, from east, n.d.
Archival Photographic Files

Mandel Hall, interior, photograph by Chicago Architectural Photographing Company, n.d. Archival Photographic Files

Adolphus C. Bartlett, photograph by Koehne of Chicago, n.d. Archival Photographic Files

rangles, but even more because Goodspeed and Harper managed to obtain it late in the spring of 1892, when the deadline for matching a pledge of $100,000 from Marshall Field was fast approaching. The son of a Vermont tanner and papermaker, Silas Cobb arrived in Chicago in 1833 with modest education and little money, but through shrewd business dealings in the saddle and harness industry he assembled a considerable fortune, including lucrative real estate holdings. Cobb made substantial investments in public utilities in Chicago and became a director of the Chicago Gas, Light and Coke Company. Later he secured positions on the boards of directors of two railroads, the Galena and Chicago Union and the Beloit and Madison, which were later combined to become the Chicago and Northwestern Railway. Cobb was also appointed the president of the Chicago City Railway Company and was responsible for introducing cable cars to the city. A potential donor to the University of Chicago because of his business success, Cobb was also drawn to the new institution's cause by overlapping family connections. His wife was the sister of Mrs. Jerome

Beecher, and after Mrs. Cobb's death he lived with his daughter and her husband, the brother of George C. Walker. Urged on by George Walker and visited in person by William Rainey Harper, Cobb agreed in June 1892 to give $150,000 to the University of Chicago, a donation that paid the construction costs of the central lecture hall already under construction.

Also salutary for the University was the offer by Adolphus Clay Bartlett in 1900 to provide $125,000 for the erection of a gymnasium on campus, galvanizing as it did the University's early emphasis on athleticism and competitive sports. Bartlett's primary personal concern in life, however, was not physical culture, on or off campus, but rather the advance of his business interests. Beginning as a lowly clerk, Bartlett was able to take advantage of generous profit-sharing measures supported by his employer, Tuttle, Hubbard and Company, so that by 1871 he had risen to become a partner in the large Chicago dry goods firm. Reflecting his new status as a city business leader,

Bartlett was appointed a member of the Chicago Board of Education in 1878, and he served on the boards of several corporations (including the powerful Northern Trust Company). Bartlett also aided in the establishment of several of the city's cultural organizations, including the Art Institute and the Chicago Historical Society, and he provided funds for the World's Parliament of Religions of 1893. In 1900, he was made a Trustee of the University, a responsibility that inspired him to supplement his initial gift to the University with $25,000 to cover additional costs incurred during the gymnasium's construction.

Leon Mandel, another prominent Chicago merchant who made a vital donation to the University of Chicago, contributed $85,000 for the construction of a much-needed assembly hall as part of the Tower Group at 57th Street and University Avenue. The son of a German Jewish dry goods retailer, Mandel was born in Kertzenheim, Germany, in 1841 and emigrated to America in 1852, where he eventually joined his brothers in Chicago to establish a department store, Mandel Brothers. A member of Chicago's Sinai Congregation, as well as a chief contributor to both the Jewish Training School and the Associated Jewish Charities of Chicago, Mandel was always alert to ways to support religious, educational, and charitable causes. He gave several thousand dollars toward the construction of Harper Memorial Library and Michael Reese Hospital, and he made provision in his will for $100,000 to be divided among a number of the city's charities upon his death.

Hull Court from south, n.d.
Archival Photographic Files

Helen Culver

The turn of the twentieth century was a time of significant expansion and change in scientific research. Great strides were being made in the campaign to discover the causes of disease. Beginning in 1901, a Nobel Prize in Physiology or Medicine was awarded annually to honor the world's leading scientists for biological research, including studies of widespread diseases such as diphtheria, malaria, lupus, and tuberculosis. Many scientific researchers were pursuing valuable work at the nation's institutions of higher learning, including the University of Chicago.

But the new University's ambition was constrained by its lack of research facilities. By the mid-1890s the University had a number of distinguished scientists on its faculty, but it lacked the facilities to provide them with supportive laboratory environments. To secure its place at the forefront of scientific research in the United States, Chicago desperately needed the resources provided by donors like Helen Culver.

While she was still rather young, Helen Culver (1832-1925) moved from her home in upstate New York to the Illinois prairie in the hopes of establishing herself as a teacher, but quickly gave up a career in education to respond to a plea for help from her cousin Charles J. Hull. Hull's wife had died in 1860, leaving him with two young children in need of a surrogate mother. Constrained by domestic expectations and feelings of familial duty, Helen took on the responsibility of raising the youngsters until their premature deaths in 1866 and 1874. Several years later, Charles Hull also died—leaving his fortune to Helen.

Over the years Helen Culver became a business associate of Hull and was partially responsible for the growth of his real estate empire. She opted not to spend her fortune on herself but rather to give it away to worthy local institutions.

She was particularly interested in Jane Addams' social reform work on the city's West Side. Learning that Addams and her colleagues needed a base of operations, she generously gave them the title to the Hull family home on Halsted Street. The reformers gratefully named their institution Hull House and made Culver one of the settlement's trustees. An advocate of efficient government and education, the reform-minded philanthropist also financed an inquiry into municipal revenues and funded University of Chicago professor W. I. Thomas's research with Florian Znaniecki on the life of Polish peasants in Europe and their immigration to America.

Perhaps the greatest example of Culver's philanthropy were her donations totaling $1.1 million to the University of Chicago. Beginning in 1895, she contributed steadily to a fund dedicated to the construction of four scientific research laboratories for zoological, botanical, anatomical, and physiological investigation. Known as the Hull Biological Laboratories, the buildings were finished in 1897 and were a symbol of Culver's personal interest in advancing research and teaching in the natural sciences. In comments at the buildings' dedicatory ceremonies, she expressed her desire to support "those forms of inquiry which explore the Creator's will as expressed in the laws of life" and to be the "means of making lives more sound and wholesome."

The Hull Court buildings did not end Culver's relationship with the University of Chicago. When reports began to circulate that the University administration was considering plans to segregate male and female students, she wrote a strongly worded letter to President William Rainey Harper in July 1902. She was prompted, she said, not "by outside influence, but by my own desire that women should have an equal chance with men for education." Gender segregation of any kind at the University of Chicago, Helen Culver believed, was absolutely unwarranted. While the University began to implement segregation for the first two years of undergraduate education, faculty and alumnae opposition to the plan was immediate and overwhelming, and the experiment was soon abandoned. Culver's generosity found final expression in a provision of her will bequeathing $600,000 from her estate to the University of Chicago.

John D. Rockefeller

The University of Chicago has long accorded John D. Rockefeller the official designation of "Founder," and that accolade may offer some historical compensation to Rockefeller's more conventional and hostile sobriquet of "robber baron." Simply put, Rockefeller's enormous contributions, totaling almost $35 million between 1892 and 1910, made possible the creation of a world-renowned research university within the short space of two decades. Although Rockefeller took great pride in the new University, he visited its campus on only two occasions—at the 1896 Quinquennial Celebration and 1901 Decennial Celebration—and each time he kept a very low profile. This modesty was in keeping with his resolute conviction that others—especially the President and the Trustees—needed to accept and to exercise responsibility for the new University. As Rockefeller's confidant and sometime advisor, Frederick Taylor Gates, put it to William

Helen Culver, n.d.
Archival Photographic Files

John D. Rockefeller, Sr., n.d.
Archival Photographic Files

Rainey Harper in 1892, "He would prefer in general not to take active part in the counsels of the management. He prefers to rest the whole weight of the management on the shoulders of the proper officers."

Rockefeller was a devoted and pious Baptist. His Christian convictions pushed him to give unstintingly to his fellow human beings, even as it tempered his giving by emphasizing the need for self-sufficiency and good work habits among those who desired his help. Born in Richford, New York, but raised in Cleveland, Ohio, Rockefeller worked his way up from clerk and bookkeeper to multimillionaire and head of the Standard Oil Company. Investments and company profits gave him an immense personal fortune, estimated by biographer Ron Chernow to be worth $200 million by

1897, but they did not bring him peace of mind, nor did they bring him admiration or respect from many Americans. If anything, his wealth became a liability; only charity, he came to believe, could put him right with God and his fellow human beings.

Rockefeller's initial philanthropic relations with the new University of Chicago were forged in 1889, when he pledged $600,000 to help launch the new university, provided that its Chicago supporters raise an additional $400,000 within a year's time. Initially, Rockefeller expected and wanted the University to be a liberal-arts college, not the research university that William Rainey Harper so strongly promoted. Moreover, he never ceased to worry that his own vast fortune would tempt his friends and compatriots in Chicago to look to him to support permanently the entire financial edifice of the University. Hence, Rockefeller was especially sensitive to the need of gaining and retaining substantial support among the members of the Chicago civic elite. In a personal meeting with Rockefeller in April 1891, Gates had found him "troubled and depressed. He has begun to feel that Chicago is lying down on him."

The great generosity soon displayed by early Chicago donors like Martin Ryerson, George Walker, Sidney Kent, Marshall Field, and others between 1891 and 1896 temporarily resolved such doubts in Rockefeller's mind, but the issue of the proper extent of his role in supporting the University continued to plague his relationships with Harper and the Board of Trustees. Moreover, Rockefeller's initial worries in 1891 and 1892 over the state of the University's finances escalated over the next decade. In his desire to attract the most distinguished research faculty to Chicago, Harper promised salaries and departmental research funds that the fledgling University could not afford.

Soon, Rockefeller found himself having to cover huge operating deficits, amounting to almost 30 per cent of the annual operating budgets between 1893 and 1904, even as Harper urged him to provide additional major gifts to the University's endowment.

After years of complaints and pleas for

John D. Rockefeller to Frederick T. Gates, manuscript letter, May 15, 1889.
University Presidents' Papers, 1889-1925.

Rockefeller Chapel, Bertram G. Goodhue, architect, J. F. Wilson, artist, architectural drawing, 1924. Archival Photographic Files

greater budgetary discipline, Rockefeller and his advisers in New York seemed determined to bring Harper under control. In late 1903 Rockefeller sent Starr J. Murphy to Chicago on an investigative mission to undertake an "exhaustive inquiry" into the University's operations and especially its finances. A no-nonsense lawyer with a sharp pen and a keen eye for the foibles of institutional budgeting, Murphy produced a long, detailed, and insightful report in early 1904 that was generally complimentary but also commented on Harper's almost charismatic power over his Trustees: "The President is a man of great persuasiveness, and it is easy for him to present to his Trustees, in a very convincing way, the importance and necessity of the things which he desires to see accomplished. Being subjected as they are to this pressure, and realizing the value and the need of the various things recommended, it is not surprising that the Trustees should be disposed to acquiesce in his plans, so far as the resources of the institution will permit; and to be optimistic with regard to the possibility of increasing those resources."

This situation, Murphy continued, must not be allowed to continue, and he left no doubt who was responsible: "The existing financial situation, and the course of financial administration for the past few years is intolerable and must be altered. While it is desirable and necessary that the Trustees should be men of broad intellectual sympathy and of keen appreciation of educational needs and possibilities, it is also necessary that they should be men of iron resolution, capable, notwithstanding their full appreciation of these things, of appreciating, with equal force, the limitations imposed by financial considerations. This is where they have proved themselves lacking, and it is in this direction that a change must be sought."

As the deficit continued to trouble Rockefeller and his advisers, Starr Murphy submitted a second, more negative report in February 1905, laying the blame on the officers of the University for the "constant and alarming increase in the budget deficits." For Murphy, the University's budget estimates were characterized by "utter worthlessness" which offered Rockefeller "no protection whatever." Indeed, they were "purely a matter of form, as the University authorities do not consider themselves in any way bound by them." The outraged reactions of Goodspeed and several other Trustees protesting against what Goodspeed called Murphy's "offensive expressions" could not mask the fact that Murphy had dared to express openly what others had only been willing to ponder silently for many years.

Starr Murphy's two reports left little doubt about the origins or the consequences of William Rainey Harper's expansionist fiscal policies, but the University was not able to curb its habits of chronic deficit spending until well after Harper's death in January 1906. Under President Harry Pratt Judson's leadership, the University finally began to exercise restraint in incurring new obligations, a change of policy that Rockefeller certainly welcomed. In the end, nevertheless, it was Rockefeller who had to resolve the deficit problem with several massive additional gifts to the endowment between 1906 and 1910, concluding with Rockefeller's Final Gift of $10 million in December 1910, his last personal University benefaction. These gifts essentially capitalized the structural deficit and allowed the University to bring order to its financial affairs without compromising its scholarly reputation or educational quality.

It has long been my purpose to set aside a portion of my estate to be used in perpetuity for the benefit of humanity. . . . After careful consideration, I concluded that the strongest guarantees of permanent and efficient administration would be assured if the property were entrusted to the University of Chicago.

Helen Culver
**Letter to the University of Chicago
Board of Trustees, 14 December 1895**

Enhancing the Campus

Annie McClure Hitchcock

At first glance, Annie McClure Hitchcock's pledge in 1899 to build a men's residence hall appears to be simply another magnanimous gesture by a local Chicago donor. Hitchcock mirrored other women donors by making a sizable donation in honor of her late spouse, Charles Hitchcock. William Rainey Harper sent her several letters thanking her profusely and then updated her on the planning of the building. Surviving letters also show that Annie Hitchcock reviewed the invitations for the hall's formal dedication ceremony before they went to their final printing. From these details emerges a portrait of an aggressive, self-willed philanthropist who knew exactly what kind of building she wanted to erect. Indeed, Hitchcock's activist style of giving not only challenged the architectural standards set by the early Trustees led by Martin Ryerson and Charles Hutchinson, it also raised the more profound question of the right of donors to participate in making policy decisions.

Annie Hitchcock (1839-1922), a native of Chicago, decided to build a permanent memorial to her husband, wealthy lawyer Charles Hitchcock, after his death in 1881. She announced in 1899 her intention to donate the funds needed to build a men's residence hall at the University of Chicago, providing $159,499 for construction and $25,000 for maintenance.

Upon learning of Annie Hitchcock's generous gift, University Trustee Charles Hutchinson, the chair of the campus planning committee of the Board, unwittingly angered Hitchcock by commissioning Charles Coolidge of the Boston architectural firm Sheply, Rutan and Coolidge to submit sketches for the building. "I am not content," Hitchcock wrote in an agitated letter to Harper, "that the building should be put up as my expression of an adequate memorial to my husband, and as my ideal of what a boy's dormitory should be, when I have not been consulted at all." Realizing that the Board of Trustees' break with architect Henry Ives Cobb in 1901 opened the way for the possibility of new architectural visions on campus, she lobbied strenuously to have the commission go instead to the rising young architect Dwight Heald Perkins. Sensing promise in Perkins, she had financed his

Annie McClure Hitchcock, n.d.
Archival Photographic Files

Hitchcock Hall, library, n.d.
Archival Photographic Files

Blaine Hall from Scammon Court, n.d. Archival Photographic Files

Anita McCormick Blaine, ca. 1883. Archival Photographic Files

education at the Massachusetts Institute of Technology; now she wished to help him further by ensuring that he would design a building to her specifications. Hitchcock had no doubt that Perkins was a wise choice—he was already working closely with some of the most progressive figures in Chicago architectural design, including Frank Lloyd Wright, Myron Hunt, and Robert C. Spencer.

Several influential Trustees resisted Hitchcock's intervention in campus planning, and they were even less enthusiastic about giving Perkins the commission. Nevertheless, Hitchcock prevailed, and the young architect set to work on the plans. Hitchcock Hall was completed September 1902 and occupied in October. It was like no other building on campus. Cloaked beneath a Gothic exterior highlighted by angular modern accents, the building's interiors blended the aesthetic of the Arts and Crafts movement with the horizontal modern style of the Prairie School. After the building's construction and occupation, Hitchcock continued her activist role in its management. She visited the residence hall frequently, and she donated carefully selected furnishings and books to elevate the social life and domestic culture of the male students it housed.

Anita McCormick Blaine

Innovations in educational thought matched those being made in science on campus in the early decades of the twentieth century. Educational reformer John Dewey's appointment to the faculty in 1894 signaled a substantial commitment by the University of Chicago to test new teaching practices and to implement new pedagogical theories. Indeed, the creation of the Laboratory School under Dewey's leadership immediately put the University on the national educational map. But to sustain Dewey's high ambitions, University administrators needed the financial resources that only a major philanthropist could provide. Into the breach stepped Anita McCormick Blaine (1866-1954). The daughter of industrialist Cyrus Hall McCormick and his wife Nettie, Blaine made a substantial gift for a building to house the University Elementary School and University High School on campus—Emmons Blaine Hall. Moreover, Blaine also provided funds to subsidize the University's programmatic work in education, a welcome expansion of the horizon of philanthropy beyond that of the first cohort of Chicago donors, whose gifts had been directed largely to building construction.

The cause of improving primary and secondary education deeply interested Anita McCormick Blaine, perhaps a reflection of the minimal education she received as a child. Believing that the existing methods of primary instruction were ineffective, Blaine searched for the

Anita McCormick Blaine to William R. Harper, manuscript letter, August 1, 1898. University Presidents' Papers, 1889-1925

right person to be her standard bearer, and she found him in Colonel Francis Wayland Parker. Since the 1870s Parker had experimented with new methods of teaching, rejecting the idea that students learned best by rote memorization. Parker's unconventional opinions (e.g., his rejection of the traditional division of subjects, his emphasis on parental involvement, and his insistence on practical learning) attracted much criticism, but Blaine became an ardent and enthusiastic supporter. In 1899 she urged Parker to establish a unique private school on the city's North Side, in which she could enroll her son Emmons, offering to fund the plan herself.

With Blaine's patronage Parker opened the Chicago Institute in 1900 in a rented German Turngemeinde, or athletic club, on North Wells Street. Plans had been developed for an impressive new building and elaborate curriculum for the Institute, but when expenses skyrocketed Blaine and Parker began to consider alternate possibilities. They found a resolution to their dilemma in a plan worked out by William Rainey Harper to incorporate the school within the University of Chicago as a part of its educational program. Blaine then announced that she would transfer her pledged investment of $700,000 in the Chicago Institute to the University of Chicago. By 1901 Blaine and Parker's enterprise had been merged with Dewey's experimental school, laying the foundations for the University's School of Education and for the modern Laboratory Schools of today. All that remained was for the new entities to receive a worthy and permanent home, which they acquired in 1904 with the completion of Emmons Blaine Hall. At the building's dedication ceremony, Blaine clarified her role in the establishment of the School of Education. "I did not found it," she affirmed. "I simply found it."

Ever a political, social, and religious non-conformist, Blaine supported a system of profit-sharing for her family's reaper business, instituted an eight-hour day for her household staff, became interested in spiritualism, and supported leftist politicians. Her endorsement of progressive Henry Wallace for President of the United States in 1948 perplexed even her closest friends and drew harsh criticism from right-wing commentators. But Anita McCormick Blaine went on to become an avid proponent of world government and international accord and remained committed to the cause for the rest of her life.

Harper Memorial Library

William Rainey Harper's death in 1906 was a severe blow to the University of Chicago community. Harper's courage, dedication, energy, and imagination had made Chicago into a distinguished research university, equal to the best universities in Europe or America. In many respects, Harper *was* the University of Chicago, and his death produced understandable and powerful anxieties about the future. Who would succeed him as President? Could that person provide the leadership to sustain Chicago's greatness while also accommodating Rockefeller's desire for budgetary probity and stability?

Harry Pratt Judson's appointment as Acting President in 1906 and as President in 1907 did not put all such anxieties to rest, but in Judson the Trustees had identified a stable, respected, if unimaginative executive who could

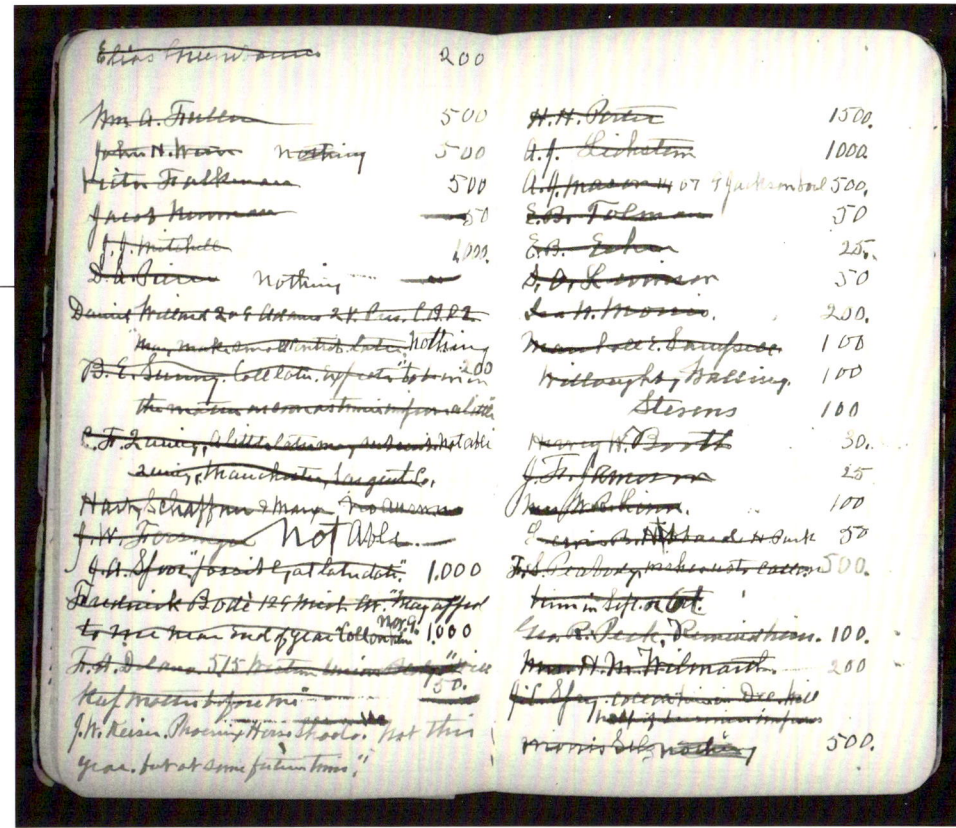

Harper Memorial Fund subscription book, manuscript, n.d. University Presidents' Papers, 1889-1925

manage the affairs of the University. One of the first major policy decisions faced by the Judson administration was the question of how the University should honor William Rainey Harper, who clearly deserved a permanent memorial on the Quadrangles. Recalling Harper's long-standing desire for a permanent library building, Judson and the Board of Trustees decided to erect a new central library in his honor.

Appropriately, John D. Rockefeller made the first and largest contribution to the fund for the Harper Memorial Library. Within a week of learning of the Trustees' decision, John D. Rockefeller, Jr. wrote to them expressing his father's support and adding that "If the Trustees favor the erecting of a University Library in memory of Dr. Harper, my father will join with the Doctor's many friends in Chicago and the East in a contribution toward it." In the end, Rockefeller's "contribution" came to no less than $600,000, almost seventy-five percent of the total cost of the building when it finally opened in 1912.

Many other donors willingly matched Rockefeller's challenge, if on a more modest scale. Indeed, the subscription list for the Library fund reads like a "who's who" of Chicago's leading philanthropists and included many of the people who gave to other programs or units of the University. Anita McCormick Blaine, Ann Swift, La Verne Noyes, Helen Culver, C. K. G. Billings, Harold Swift, Julius Rosenwald, Catherine Seipp, and Frances Lillie each gave between $500 and $5,000 to the cause, while Martin Ryerson offered $25,000. National philanthropists such as Andrew Carnegie contributed, as did many University of Chicago alumni. Faculty members and students were also extremely generous, with faculty donations totaling almost $14,000

Harper Memorial Library, laying of the cornerstone, n.d. Archival Photographic Files

Harper Memorial Library, construction, October 1, 1910. Archival Photographic Files

and the Classes of 1904 and 1905 channeling their Class gifts toward the memorial. By the time construction on the building actually began in 1910, over two thousand University supporters had contributed to the Harper Memorial Fund. While diverse in so many other ways, all of these donors were united in their admiration for William Rainey Harper and the extraordinary work that he had accomplished.

LaVerne Noyes

Windmills and wire dictionary holders may have generated the money that built Ida Noyes Hall, but the conviction that women and men should have equal access to services on the University of Chicago campus gave the building its real meaning. Before La Verne Noyes gave $500,000 in 1913 to erect the elegant building, men and women students had resided in separate (and unequal) social worlds. Although the University was founded as a coeducational institution, tendencies toward gender inequality were evident early on. When Reynolds Club (1903) and Bartlett Gymnasium (1904) were opened, the University restricted their use to male students. For group meetings and larger social gatherings, women students had only the inadequate quarters of Lexington Hall, a "temporary" brick building erected north of the President's House as part of the University's ill-fated gender segregation scheme.

Born in Genoa, New York, La Verne Noyes (1849-1919) moved with his family to Iowa as a small boy and attended Cornell College in Mt. Vernon, Iowa. He began his career as an inventor when he went to work as a laboratory technician at Ames Agricultural College (now Iowa State University). He eventually left his job at the college and went into business for himself by producing and marketing machines and devices of his own invention. In 1877 Noyes married Ida E. Smith, and one of his most successful products resulted from Ida's difficulty in holding their heavy unabridged Webster's dictionary—Noyes designed a wire dictionary holder to aid his new bride, and soon patented the device for sales throughout the United States. Noyes's most lucrative invention came in 1886, however. This was the aëromotor, a device that converted wind to electricity and proved to be immensely useful to American farmers in the late nineteenth century.

In 1879, the Noyeses moved to Chicago. With the success of La Verne's business enterprises over the next thirty years, the couple was able to lead a progressively more comfortable life and establish their residence in an elegant mansion at 1450

LaVerne Noyes, n.d. Archival Photographic Files

30

Masque of Youth Processional, performance for the opening of Ida Noyes Hall, 1916. Archival Photographic Files

North Lake Shore Drive. Ida enjoyed traveling around the world, spending months at a time away from Chicago and her husband. She wrote him often from such exotic places as Paris, Jerusalem, and Hawaii. Noyes would occasionally join her on these trips, but his manufacturing business made it difficult to leave the city for extended periods of time. As his wealth grew, Noyes began to make substantial contributions to local charities such as the United Charities, the Park Ridge School for Girls, the Country Home for Convalescent Children, the local YMCA hotel, and the Chicago Half-Orphan Asylum. He also donated $10,000 in 1915 to create a reservoir on the campus of Iowa State in Ames, Iowa, which was named Lake La Verne.

Ida Noyes's sudden and unexpected death in December 1912 dealt La Verne Noyes a crushing personal blow. Seeking to honor his wife with an impressive and fitting memorial, he decided within six months of her death to give the University of Chicago a gift of $500,000 to build a magnificent new women's clubhouse. Dedicated on June 5, 1916, during the University's twenty-fifth anniversary celebration, Ida Noyes Hall was a splendid tribute to his wife's memory. Each year thereafter Noyes invited a group of senior undergraduate women students to his home for a special luncheon in their honor. Finally, in his last and most extraordinary gift, Noyes established the La Verne Noyes Foundation at the University in July 1918. With this foundation Noyes provided tuition scholarships to veterans of World War I and to their descendants. To finance this endowment, Noyes in the year before his death deeded all of his property, including his home and his manufacturing plant, to the University of Chicago—a gift worth $2.5 million.

Ida Noyes Hall, entrance, photograph by Capes, 1938. Archival Photographic Files

31

Julius Rosenwald, photograph by Atlantic Foto Service, Atlantic City, n.d. Archival Photographic Files

Julius Rosenwald

When Booker T. Washington called upon African Americans to gain formal education and work toward self-reliance, wealthy white progressives were spurred to provide America's black population with financial as well as rhetorical support. In the 1920s a number of American philanthropists, including Chicago's Julius Rosenwald, dedicated themselves to the challenge of confronting the unsolved national problem of racial inequality. Persuaded by Washington's concept of racial uplift, Rosenwald funded construction of 5,357 rural schools and related buildings for Southern blacks, ensured the construction and equipping of YMCAs open to all races, and served as trustee of the Tuskegee Institute in Alabama. He also gave thousands of dollars to progressive reform organizations such as Chicago's Hull House, supported medical care for Chicago's African-Americans through donations to Provident Hospital, and in 1929 built a low-income housing complex for the city's African-American populace. "Race prejudice is merely destructive," he said in an address to the American Missionary Association in 1911, because "it offers nothing but a hopeless warfare and a blank pessimism."

Born to Jewish immigrant parents in Springfield, Illinois, Julius Rosenwald (1862-1932) attained great financial and political power as president (1910-24) and chairman of the board (1924-32) of Sears, Roebuck and Company. A careful and judicious donor who gave in the hope that others would do likewise, Rosenwald was an ardent advocate of a conception of philanthropy that focused on expendable rather than endowment resources. He published newspaper and magazine essays arguing that donors had a responsibility to make sure that their contributions were most effective in their own time, leaving the needs of the future to the generosity of donors who would surely come later. In a January 1929 *Saturday Evening Post* article he declared "that the needs of the future can safely be left to be met by the generations of the future... Like the manna of the Bible, which melted at the close of each day, philanthropic enterprises should come to an end with the close of the philanthropist's life." Funds for worthy causes should be given in a donor's lifetime, rather than by creating permanent foundations, because the subsequent administrative leaders of such foundations could easily ignore the original intentions of the donor. Each generation, Rosenwald firmly believed, was responsible for solving its own social problems.

Yet, even as Julius Rosenwald confronted some of the thorniest social policy dilemmas of his time, he also supported the cause of quality private higher education with magnificent gifts to the University of Chicago. Like his close neighbors

Tuskegee Institute Board of Trustees, n.d. Seated third and fourth from left in front row are Rosenwald and Booker T. Washington respectively. Julius Rosenwald Papers

Burton-Judson Courts, construction, photograph by Chicago Architectural Photographing Company, May 4, 1931. Archival Photographic Files

plemented that gift in 1925 with a million-dollar donation to be assigned at the discretion of his fellow Trustees, and in 1928 he pledged $2 million toward the cost of erecting Burton-Judson Courts, the elegant residence halls for men located just across the Midway. An additional $250,000 gift from Rosenwald supported construction of the new Chicago Lying-In Hospital in the University's growing medical center.

and fellow Trustees Martin Ryerson and Harold Swift, Rosenwald maintained a residence just north of the University in the Kenwood neighborhood, where he owned a grand, if cumbersome mansion at 4901 S. Ellis Avenue. Like Ryerson and Swift, residential proximity to the University became one of many reasons for Rosenwald to give so generously. For such civic leaders the new University of Chicago was not only "Chicago's University," but also Kenwood's and Hyde Park's university as well.

Rosenwald's first donation came in 1904, when he contributed $6,500 to purchase the collection of German literary works that came to be known as the Hirsch-Bernays Library. Soon after his appointment to the Board of Trustees in 1912, Rosenwald surprised his fellow Trustees by pledging $250,000 to erect a building to house the University's Geography Department, Rosenwald Hall. Funds needed to build a library for the University's research center in Luxor, Egypt, followed, and in 1916 Rosenwald gave $500,000 to help launch the University's new medical school. He sup-

Burton-Judson Courts, dining hall, photograph by Capes Photo, n.d. Archival Photographic Files

Again, you will do well to remember that success consists not in getting but in giving. In this somewhat materialistic age emphasis is too often on getting. The value of getting knowledge, power, possessions, influence is only that they may be used in some helpful way for others.

John D. Rockefeller, Jr.
"On Behalf of the Founder,"
Remarks made at the Ninety-ninth
Convocation, 6 June 1916

Supporting Research and Learning

Scholarships, Fellowships, Lectureships, and Prizes

Early endowments for student scholarships, graduate fellowships, and faculty lectureships were essential in establishing the University's reputation as a place of lively scholarly inquiry accessible to the most gifted students and faculty. After World War I, University administrators could look back at these first donations as worthy precursors to the major gifts raised for the support of academic and student-life programs that were at the heart of the development campaign of 1924-26.

University Trustees were among those making gifts for fellowships, scholarships, and research prizes. Charles L. Hutchinson, for example, established a fellowship fund to support teaching and research in Latin in 1893. Born in 1854, Hutchinson was still a child when his family moved to the frontier town of Chicago from their home in Lynn, Massachusetts. His father Benjamin ensured the financial success of his family by founding lucrative businesses in meatpacking, banking, and the grain trade, becoming a major figure in the Chicago business community of the 1870s and 1880s. When he reached maturity, the younger Hutchinson used his share of his father's fortune, along with the considerable resources generated from his work as president of the Corn Exchange Bank, to establish himself as one of the most influential and inspired leaders of cultural philanthropy in Chicago in the late nineteenth century.

Although he never attended college, Hutchinson was passionately interested in the fine arts, and in 1882, at the age of 28, he was tapped to be president of the Art Institute, serving until his death in 1934. In the fall of 1890 Hutchinson played a pivotal role in the successful founding of the new University by offering Frederick Gates and Thomas Goodspeed his personal support during their fundraising canvas among non-Baptist Chicago civic leaders. In the months that followed, Hutchinson's good name and solid reputation opened many doors that would have otherwise remained closed. Appropriately, Charles Hutchinson was named along with his close friend Martin Ryerson as a member of the first Board of Trustees of the new University of Chicago. He proved a dedicated supporter and found a special role as the chairman of the Trustees' Committee on Buildings and Grounds, which allowed him to exercise supervisory control over many of the most important construction projects in the first thirty years of University's history. In 1901 Hutchinson gave the University $60,000 for the construction of Hutchinson Commons, a central dining hall in the neo-Gothic Tower Group, whose design and planning gave great delight to the capitalist connoisseur.

Other Chicagoans soon followed Hutchinson by supporting research and teaching opportunities at the University. One such donor, Caroline Haskell, gave $40,000 in 1894 to endow two extraordinary programs—the Haskell and the Barrows Lectureships on Comparative Religion. Committed to Christianity's missionary spirit but also intensely curious about non-Christian religions as a result of having attended the World's Parliament of Religions in 1893, Haskell wanted her lectureships to encourage the interest that late-nineteenth-century Americans were beginning to show in Eastern religions. Haskell also prescribed that the Barrows Lectures were to be delivered in India, where her lecturers would present the "great questions of the truths of Christianity, its harmonies

Charles L. Hutchinson, n.d.
Archival Photographic Files

Horace Spencer Fiske, photograph by Moffett Russell, n.d. Archival Photographic Files

Announcement Concerning the Conrad Seipp Memorial German Prizes, printed pamphlet, n.d. University Presidents' Papers, 1889-1925

with the truths of other religions, its rightful claims, and the best methods of setting them forth," to the "scholarly and thoughtful people of India." Caroline Haskell's third and final donation of 1894 was a $100,000 gift to erect the Haskell Oriental Museum on the University campus. The cornerstone of this building, which now houses the Department of Anthropology, proclaims what might be considered one of Mrs. Haskell's fundamental ideals, *Lux ex oriente*, "Light from the East."

Like Caroline Haskell, Catherine Seipp leavened research-oriented contributions to the University with her own vision of Chicago's intellectual priorities. The wife of one of Chicago's best-known German-American brewers, Seipp was interested in calling attention to the issue of ethnic identity and the place it deserved in scholarly research. In 1904 she presented the University with $6,000 to establish the Conrad Seipp Memorial German Prizes. Named for her husband, the three one-time prizes honored the best monographs submitted on the topic, "The German Element in the United States with Special Reference to Its Political, Moral, Social, and Educational Influence."

Less wealthy men and women did what they could to bolster the cause of higher education at the University of Chicago. Charles Smiley's gift demonstrated such a commitment in a remarkable way. An African-American who grew up in impoverished circumstances, Smiley rose into Chicago's lower middle class by operating a catering business on the city's South Side. According to his friend and University Trustee Jesse Baldwin, the popularity of this business enterprise brought Smiley financial prosperity. Of the entrepreneur's $11,000 estate at the time of his death in 1911, $3,000 was set aside to endow the Charles H. Smiley Scholarship at the University of Chicago, yielding $150 a year. Smiley's express wish was that the scholarship should be used to provide support for "poor but promising students, preferably of the colored race."

Staff members such as Horace Spencer Fiske also made gifts of prizes to the University. Seeking to recognize the artistic abilities of graduate and undergraduate students, Fiske gave a thousand-dollar bond to President Harry Pratt Judson in 1919 to establish the John Billings Fiske Prize in Poetry. He then doubled the fund in 1936. A onetime lecturer in the University Extension and retired editor of both the *University Record* and *The University of Chicago Magazine*, Fiske established the prize to honor his late father. While the prize fund's annual return was a rather modest fifty dollars, students were drawn by the chance to have the winning work published in the *University Record*. Marian Esther Manly, an undergraduate student who was the daughter of Methodist missionaries, received the first John Billings Fiske Prize in 1920 for her poem, "Li Sien."

Howard Taylor Ricketts

Public rites marking the death of pathologist Howard T. Ricketts in 1910 commemorated an extraordinary scholarly life, lived to the full. Foreign dignitaries moved by Ricketts' campaigns against disease placed honorary ribbons on his casket. Grieving members of the scientific community named both a taxonomic family (*Rickettsiaceae*) and an order (*Rick-*

The University of Chicago
FOUNDED BY JOHN D. ROCKEFELLER

Announcement

Concerning the CONRAD SEIPP MEMORIAL GERMAN PRIZES

FOUNDED BY MRS. CATHERINE SEIPP

1) Three Prizes are proposed for the three best monographs upon the subject: "The German Element in the United States with Special Reference to its Political, Moral, Social, and Educational Influence."

2) The prizes are to be in sums of $3,000, $2,000, and $1,000.

3) The monographs are to be delivered to the German department of The University of Chicago on or before the 22d of March, 1907.

4) The monographs may be written in either English or German; the monograph selected for publication shall be printed in English, possibly also in German.

Howard T. Ricketts in
Mexico City laboratory, n.d.
Howard Taylor Ricketts Papers

Maud Slye to David A. Robertson,
manuscript letter, May 7, 1915.
University Presidents' Papers, 1889-1925

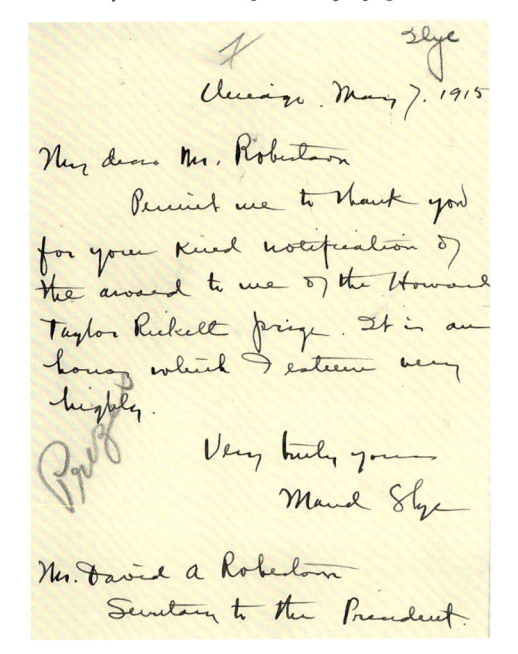

ettsiales) after him. But the most meaningful memorial to Ricketts may have been the student research prize his family established in his honor. While Ricketts's wife and children, like most faculty families, were unable to make a large donation owing to their rather modest means, they hoped to encourage the pursuit of new knowledge that had been the focus of Ricketts' scientific life.

Howard Taylor Ricketts (1871-1910) was a native Midwesterner and a Northwestern University medical graduate. Fascinated by the study of disease but unwilling to restrict himself to traditional research methods, Ricketts sometimes injected himself with pathogens as a way of measuring their effects. This unorthodox approach, combined with his work on blastomycosis (a fungal infection that normally affects the skin), merited him a teaching offer in 1901 from the Department of Pathology and Bacteriology at the University of Chicago. Before he formally accepted the offer, Ricketts took time off to study at the Pasteur Institute in Paris. Arriving in Chicago in 1902, he continued his study of blastomycosis and in 1904 was appointed assistant to John M. Dodson, the University's dean of medical students.

While at the University of Chicago, Ricketts planned an investigation of Rocky Mountain spotted fever, and in 1906, with funding from the McCormick Memorial Institute, the State of Montana, the University, and the American Medical Association, he traveled to Montana to study the disease. For the next four years, Ricketts divided his life between campus-based laboratories and his research in the field. As part of his research, he contacted victims of the disease, collected and studied affected animals, and raised additional funds for his project. Not until the second year of his investigation, however, did Ricketts and his assistant J. J. Moore make a critical breakthrough by discovering that wood ticks were the primary carriers of the bacillus that caused the fever.

An outbreak of typhus in Mexico City caught Ricketts's attention, and taking advantage of a leave of absence from the University of Chicago and relying on the principles he had established in his Montana research, Ricketts went to Mexico in 1909 and plunged into his study of typhus. There he discovered that typhus closely resembled spotted fever, leading him to argue that insects spread both diseases. Unknown to Ricketts, this same conclusion had been reached by the French surgeon Jules Henri Nicolle, who identified lice as the culprits. Ricketts's final stint of research was cut short by a critical illness. Just days after isolating the microorganism he contended was the cause of typhus, Ricketts died on May 5, 1910, most likely from an infected insect's bite.

As a memorial to her husband, Myra Tubbs Ricketts in 1912 donated $5,000 to the University. She stipulated that the income from the endowment was to go to providing an annual prize—the Howard Taylor Ricketts Prize—for "the student presenting the best results of research in Pathology or Bacteriology." Others who were moved to memorialize Ricketts raised money to build a laboratory in his honor for the Department of Pathology, Hygiene, and Bacteriology.

38

Named the Ricketts Laboratory, the building was erected in 1914 and stood on Ellis Avenue until its site was claimed more than seventy years later by the Kersten Physics Teaching Center and the gate to the Science Quadrangle.

Jesse L. and Susan Colver Rosenberger

According to campus folklore, Jesse L. Rosenberger was a generous recluse who walked Chicago's streets with a strange request, written on a small card, tucked inside his coat pocket. The card directed whomever might find Rosenberger's body to fulfill his last request, namely, that the University of Chicago must be notified immediately about his death. This puzzling dictum was all the more ironic in view of the fact that after the death of Rosenberger's wife in 1918, he avoided any personal contact with University officials.

Jesse L. (1860-1939) and Susan Colver Rosenberger (1859-1918) came from very different family backgrounds. A descendant of a long line of Baptist preachers, Susan was born a New England Yankee. Jesse, on the other hand, counted among his ancestors German Mennonites from Pennsylvania; he was so intrigued by his heritage that he published three books with the University of Chicago Press on the Pennsylvania Germans and the Colver and Rosenberger families. Yet the Rosenbergers' early lives did have powerful similarities as well, for each had been born to parents given to constant moves, and each learned to endure incessant displacement as a child. Both were teachers at some point in their lives, and they shared the distinction of attending the first University of Chicago. Although Jesse was forced to finish his education at the University of Rochester when the University of Chicago entered bankruptcy, Susan was able to complete her bachelor's (1882) and master's (1886) degrees at the Old University. Trained as a lawyer at the Chicago College of Law of Lake Forest University, Rosenberger set up a law practice in 1890 and eventually made a substantial fortune by publishing law and business journals.

Jesse and Susan first became acquainted through the professional association of their fathers, but their relationship

Jesse L. Rosenberger, n.d. Archival Photographic Files

blossomed on the University campus. The couple wed in 1912, but their marital bliss was short-lived. Susan began suffering from periodic nervous exhaustion and rheumatism soon after their wedding, forcing Jesse to close his law and publishing offices so they could travel to more congenial climates in an effort to improve her health. In 1918 the Rosenbergers returned to Chicago, only to learn that Susan had developed a brain tumor. She died on November 19, 1918, from complications associated with surgery.

Loyal alumni of the Old University,

Susan Esther Colver Rosenberger, photograph reproduced from Jesse L. Rosenberger, *Through Three Centuries: Colver and Rosenberger, Lives and Times, 1620-1922*. Chicago: University of Chicago Press, 1922. University of Chicago Press Imprint Collection

Frank W. Gunsaulus, photograph by Walinger, n.d. Archival Photographic Files

John Marshall to Daniel Webster, manuscript letter, May 20, 1826. Butler-Gunsaulus Collection

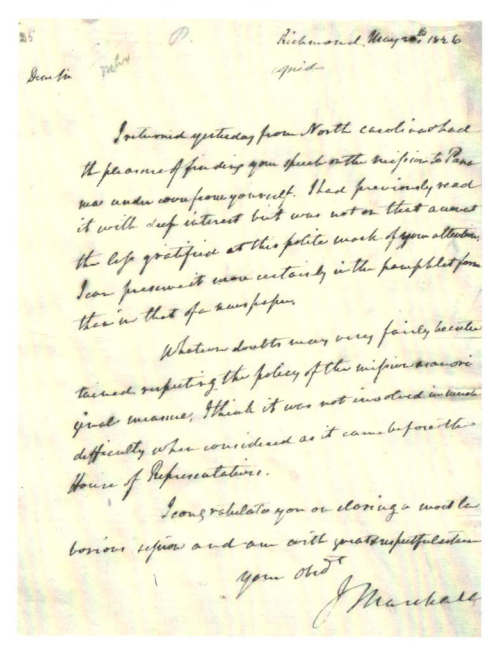

the Rosenbergers were no less staunch champions of its successor. Over the course of 23 years, they gave $55,000 to the University, beginning with the transfer in 1915 of an old homestead owned by Susan's grandfather, Nathaniel Colver. The sale of this property created the Nathaniel Colver Lectureship and Publication Fund. Two months later, the couple gave an additional gift to establish the Colver-Rosenberger Lecture Fund, and continued to make substantial gifts for fellowships, scholarships, and other forms of student aid over the next several years. In 1917 they made a gift of $3,000 to fund a University-wide prize, the Rosenberger Medal. Created to honor outstanding scholarly and artistic efforts, the Medal constitutes one of the highest honors the University can bestow. Over the years the University has awarded the Rosenberger Medal to such distinguished individuals as author Toni Morrison, conductors Sir Georg Solti and Pierre Boulez, and Frederick Grant Banting, the discoverer of insulin.

Jesse Rosenberger continued to give generously to the University in memory of his late wife. As late as 1938, just a year before his death, he gave thousands of dollars to endow two permanent funds known as the Susan Colver Rosenberger Aid Fund and the Susan Colver Rosenberger Educational Prize. The Aid Fund financed gifts or loans to students—especially women—who were preparing to teach or enter the field of social work, while the Prize funded awards for superior dissertation research in education.

Frank W. Gunsaulus

During the first decades of the twentieth century, American rare book and manuscript collecting became a fashionable pursuit that offered intellectual and cultural satisfactions as well as the camaraderie of fellow devotees. Chicago's Caxton Club, founded in 1895, along with informal social gatherings, provided an opportunity for bibliophiles to share their love of books. A group of collectors who regularly haunted the rare book section of Alexander C. McClurg's bookstore were dubbed "Saints and Sinners" by humorist Eugene Field, one of the regulars. Among the clerical members of the group was Frank Wakeley Gunsaulus (1856-1921), who was perhaps the most notable Chicago collector to contribute rare books, manuscripts, and autographs to the early University of Chicago. Born in Chesterville, Ohio, Gunsaulus came to prominence as the minister of the socially prestigious Plymouth Congregational Church of Chicago. Gunsaulus extended his reputation as a powerful preacher and earned extra money to support his book and manuscript collecting by conducting summer lecture tours across the country.

Influenced by deep religious principles, Gunsaulus, like other culturally conservative reformers in America and in Europe, hoped that a robust program of philanthropy could alleviate, if not eliminate, the worst aspects of modern life. One outlet for Gunsaulus's cultural and social revisionism was his own personal crusade to create new, more egalitarian educational institutions. In an address to his Plymouth Church parishioners, he proposed founding an institute of technology that would be open to all qualified students seeking technical training. Inspired by Gunsaulus's idea, meatpacking magnate Philip D. Armour put up the needed money to launch the Armour Institute of Technology in 1893, an institution Gunsaulus served for the rest of his life as president (and which later became the Illinois Institute of Technology). Gunsaulus assumed a second academic position in 1912, when he was appointed Professorial Lecturer on Practical Theology in the University of Chicago Divinity School.

For Gunsaulus, collecting and reading antiquarian books and manuscripts was another way to escape the materialism and immorality of modernity. Eugene Field's story, "The Temptation of Friar Gonsol," written in 1889, recounts how Friar Gonsol (Gunsaulus) and Friar Francis (Frank W. Bristol) were tempted by a rare book. Gunsaulus believed that, confronted with the power and aesthetic appeal of texts from the past, readers would naturally be encouraged to renew themselves intellectually and spiritually. The aged pages of a manuscript had an almost magical power to recall a world where values such as chivalric honor were still meaningful. Nor was this journey back in time to be the privilege of a wealthy few. Gunsaulus saw it as his personal mission to provide manuscripts and rare books to the University of Chicago, so it could become a present-day repository of the creative achievements of past centuries. Visitors to the University Library, "weary of vulgar and soul-destroying success" and pining for a return to "knightly devotion to what often seem lost causes in politics, society, church, and state," would gain enlightenment from viewing his gifts.

Despite his loyalty to the Armour Institute, Gunsaulus reserved his most valuable gifts for the University of Chicago, prompting library administrator J.C.M. Hanson to dub him "the patron saint of the University Libraries." In 1910 Gunsaulus gave the Library a large number of early American manuscripts, letters, and autographs (eventually known as the Butler-Gunsaulus Collection). Two years later, he began to donate medieval and Renaissance manuscripts and early printed books, his most significant donations coming between 1915 and 1917. In these two years, Gunsaulus presented a manuscript of Boccaccio's *Genealogia deorum gentilium* (1385-87), and early printed editions of Augustine's *De civitate dei* (1470) and Cicero's *De officiis* (1470). Gunsaulus also donated a copy of the St. Albans *Chronicle* (1481), still regarded as one of the finest specimens of early English typography in the United States. Gunsaulus concluded his gifts to the University in 1917 and 1919 with additional fifteenth-century books and the proof sheets for Felix Mendelssohn's oratorio *Elijah*, annotated by the composer.

Giovanni Boccaccio. *Genealogia deorum gentilium*, 1385-1387, MS 100. Gift of Frank W. Gunsaulus. Codex Manuscript Collection. (detail)

Henry Fletcher. *The Perfect Politician*. London: Printed by J. Cottrel for William Roybould, 1660. The George Morris Eckels Collection, Presented by Mrs. George M. Eckels. Rare Book Collection

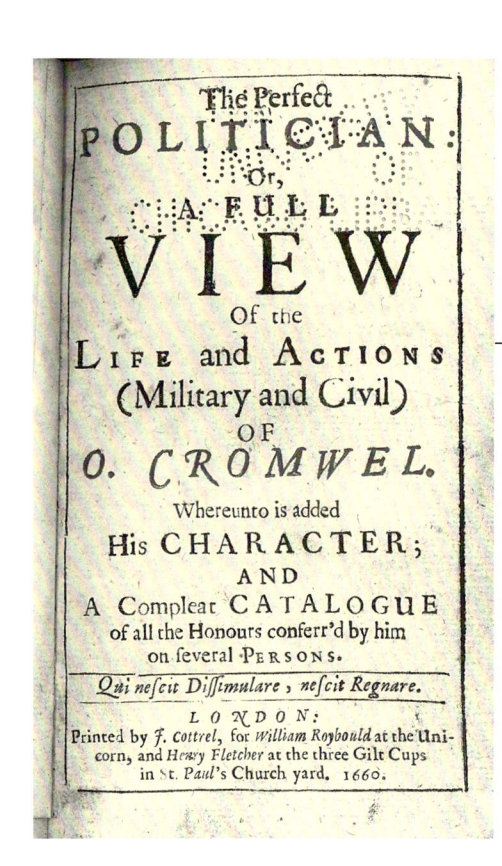

Enriching the University Library

Unlike donors who provide funds for buildings, scholarships, and the purchase of library materials, private individuals who present books and manuscripts to an institution have personal as well as philanthropic goals. Collectors who have acquired materials with purpose and passion often wish to preserve the integrity of their collection and see that it serves educational and scholarly uses.

One gift to the University of Chicago Library, made at the suggestion of Charles L. Hutchinson, was the only book collection to have survived the Chicago fire and be preserved under one roof. The Ebenezer Lane Library was started by lawyer and judge Ebenezer Lane (1793-1866), who arrived in Chicago in 1856 from Ohio and served as counsel and resident director of the Illinois Central Railroad. His son, Ebenezer S. Lane (1819-1892), graduated from Kenyon College and then studied medicine at the Ohio Medical School and in Paris. He left the practice of medicine to work in the railroad, real estate and loan business; and he also followed his father's interest in collecting books, manuscripts, and autographs. The Lane collection totaled about 10,000 volumes when his children, the third Ebenezer Lane and his daughter, Fannie G. Lane, began discussions about presenting it to the University of Chicago, along with family papers. The collection, now dispersed throughout Special Collections and the Library's circulating stacks, brought important works in history, travel, topography, science, art, architecture, and literature to the University at a time when faculty interests were expanding into new areas of concentration.

Because collectors often constitute a closely knit community, decisions about the disposition of a collection can influence others in the circle. Few Library donors did more than Gunsaulus to extend their own contributions by persuading their friends to contribute. Knowing of the strong tradition of biblical study at the University, Chicago collector Emma B. Hodge made a series of gifts between 1912 and 1920 of early printed books and manuscripts of the Renaissance and Reformation period, so that they would be available to students and scholars. Her gifts included works written or containing commentary by Erasmus, Luther, and Philip Melancthon. Scholarship has concluded that marginal

Elizabeth Day McCormick Apocalypse. Bible, New Testament, Revelation, 17th century. MS 931. Gift of Elizabeth Day McCormick. Edgar J. Goodspeed Collection

George M. Eckels, in study, n.d.
Gift of Virginia Eckels Malone.
Archival Photographic Files

commentary in two books previously believed to have been owned and annotated by Melancthon are more likely to have been written by members of the Grynaeus family of humanists, illustrating the way that books in the Hodge collection continue to stimulate research and investigation.

Also at Gunsaulus's suggestion, Mrs. Erskine M. Phelps donated her late husband's Napoleon collection to the University in 1910. Phelps's husband had been passionate about collecting everything and anything associated with Napoleon. By the end of his life he had acquired seventy-five objets d'art, ninety-five books, three autograph documents, an assortment of objects including Napoleon's spectacles, and a lock of the general's hair.

Gifts to the University Library from Chicago collectors demonstrated confidence in the University's progress and a desire to support its educational and research program. In 1916, Mrs. George M. Eckels presented to the University the collection of books and other materials relating to Oliver Cromwell and the Puritan Commonwealth formed by her late husband, Chicago lawyer George M. Eckels. The collection, consisting of over 500 books, pamphlets, engravings and other materials, was considered to be the most complete at that time for the study of this turbulent period in English history. In her letter to President Judson, Mrs. Eckels explained that "While Mr. Eckels had no official connection with the University, he followed its development with enthusiastic interest, and I feel that placing this material at the disposal of students of the University engaged in broad and thorough research is an expression, in concrete form, of that interest, and the best of memorials to him."

New Testament scholarship at the University resulted in a number of dramatic manuscript acquisitions to support the textual, iconographic, linguistic and historical research of Edgar J. Goodspeed and others. In 1932 Goodspeed discovered a complete thirteenth-century Byzantine New Testament manuscript in a Paris antique shop that was acquired by Goodspeed's colleague Harold R. Willoughby for Mrs. Edith Rockefeller McCormick and loaned to the Department of New Testament for study. The Rockefeller McCormick New Testament was purchased by Elizabeth Day McCormick, daughter of Anita McCormick Blaine's cousin Robert, from her cousin's estate in 1942 and donated to the University. Elizabeth Day McCormick also acquired a unique illustrated manuscript of Revelation in Greek, dated ca. 1600. She made the manuscript available to University scholars and in 1937 presented the Elizabeth Day McCormick Apocalpyse to the University.

Not all Library donors were wealthy members of the city's establishment. A young Polish-American post office employee, Stansilaw Jan Figura, also sought to emulate the example of earlier benefactors. Starting with a few Polish-language pamphlets in 1934, Figura donated more than 200 books to the University Library over the next twenty-five years, purchasing them on his meager U.S. postal clerk's salary.

We are, however, human enough to feel deeply stirred by the appreciation that the gift of the Whitman Laboratory has brought forth.... It stands for our belief that research is the highest function of the University and for our abiding affection for the institution in which so great a part of our active life has been spent.

Frank R. Lillie

**Remarks at the Dedication of
Whitman Laboratory, 4 June 1926**

Expanding University Resources

The University Campaign of 1924-26

The University of Chicago's development campaign of 1924-26 was the brainchild of President Ernest DeWitt Burton. A long-time faculty member in the Divinity School, Burton had occupied various administrative leadership positions during the Harper and Judson presidencies, including the Directorship of the University Library. When Judson decided to retire in late 1922, and the pool of external candidates to succeed him proved unpromising, the Board of Trustees turned to Burton to become the third President of the University. Any notion that Burton's tenure would be merely "acting" soon disappeared. In the early months of his administration, demonstrating energetic leadership that had been woefully missing from the last five years of Judson's presidency, Burton began to conceive a broad-based fundraising effort to meet the University's financial needs.

Burton's strong leadership was desperately needed, for the early 1920s were a time of great challenges and perplexing transitions for the University. Not only had John D. Rockefeller's largesse finally come to a close with receipt of the last installment of his Final Gift in January 1920, but Chicago was encountering serious competitive challenges from Harvard, Columbia, and other leading research universities in retaining distinguished senior faculty and in recruiting the most promising younger researchers. By the mid-1920s Columbia's top salary levels for its most distinguished full professors exceeded the University of Chicago's salary range by almost 20 per cent. Similar disparities occurred in the ranks of associate and assistant professor. Chicago required serious new investments in faculty compensation, but it also needed substantial new funds to support faculty research. As the most senior faculty from the Harper and Judson eras began to retire, the University faced the need to recruit a new generation of distinguished researchers to Hyde Park. Moreover, a massive post-war surge in student enrollments (Chicago had 13,000 students in 1924, compared to 6,000 in 1910) had put heavy pressure on facilities and instructional resources alike. Additionally, the ambitious plans for the new Medical School, which had languished during World War I, now needed to be implemented.

During February and March of 1924, Burton and his associates conducted a detailed survey of current and future University needs and concluded that the University needed to double its endowment within the next ten to fifteen years, which meant adding $55 million in new capital resources, with at least $17.5 million of this money being raised within the next two years. Working closely

Committee on Development, 1924. Standing from left to right: A. A. Stagg, Helen Norris, Arthur C. Bestor, Alice Greenacre, H. F. Zimmerman. Seated from left to right: Harold H. Swift, President Ernest D. Burton, and John P. Mentzer. Archival Photographic Files

THE PLAN FOR DEVELOPMENT OF THE UNIVERSITY OF CHICAGO

PRELIMINARY STATEMENT ISSUED BY
THE COMMITTEE ON DEVELOPMENT
1703 LYTTON BUILDING CHICAGO

I

THE PROGRAM OF DEVELOPMENT

The University of Chicago occupies an exceptional position among the great universities of the world. It is the youngest and one of the largest; it has been termed one of the most original. Starting from nothing more tangible than an idea in 1889, the University last year gave instruction to 13,359 students. Every State in the Union, three Territories, and thirty-four foreign countries were represented in the enrollment. Rising from nothing better than hopes in 1889, the University possessed last June an endowment of $31,992,620.76, — the fourth largest among the universities of the country. In a third of a century The University of Chicago has made for itself a position in the educational life of America equalled by few institutions, regardless of age.

Committee on Development, "The Plan for Development of the University of Chicago," 1925. University Development Campaigns and Anniversaries Records

---

with Board President Harold Swift, Burton also determined that a fundraising campaign of such magnitude and scope—well beyond anything ever attempted in the Harper era—compelled the University to seek the advice and managerial expertise of outside professionals. Hence, in May 1924 the Trustees commissioned the John Price Jones Corporation of New York to oversee the first professionally directed fundraising campaign in the University's history. The Trustees further agreed upon a two-year campaign goal of $6.5 million for new buildings and $11 million for additional endowment in support of faculty salaries, facilities, research, and student life. Burton's leadership was to be critical to the success or failure of the campaign. His elegant brochure, *The University of Chicago in 1940*, produced in 1925 to provide an overall vision for the campaign, was and remains one of the most ambitious and coherent fundraising visions ever articulated by a President of the University.

The campaign of 1924-26 was a remarkable effort. Under the tutelage of the Jones Corporation, University officials moved beyond the traditional range of donors relied upon in the past—the members of the Board of Trustees and other selected major gift prospects—to include the University's alumni and friends and even its faculty as potential donors. An extensive network of alumni groups based throughout the United States raised $1.9 million, based on contributions from no less than 11,300 alumni, a remarkable achievement for a university most of whose graduates were not yet in positions of wealth and influence. The Rockefeller-funded General Education Board added an additional $2 million, while the University's Trustees raised close to $1.7 million within their own ranks.

Prominent Chicagoans also gave generously, both toward construction of new buildings such as Wieboldt Hall and to the creation of new endowments for research and teaching, including particularly the new Distinguished Service Professorships that were one of Burton's most treasured initiatives. The first such Professorship was funded by Martin Ryerson in 1925 with a gift of $200,000, and his generosity was matched in the next several years by Frank P. Hixon, Charles H. Swift, Sewell L. Avery, Charles F. Grey, Morton D. Hull, and others. In all, the University's development effort raised $7 million in a year and a half.

Burton's untimely death on May 26, 1925, was a crushing blow to the campaign. As the final report on the campaign put it with quiet elegance, "Many alumni and citizens of Chicago believed in him and were willing to follow where he led." Inheriting a campaign that had temporarily lost its momentum, and uncomfortable with the strategies proposed by the professional fundraisers, the new President of the University, Max Mason, decided in January 1926 to conclude the University's contractual relationship with the John Price Jones Corporation and pursue institutional development in a less public manner. By 1928, Mason's "quiet" campaign had brought the total amount raised to $12 million of the original $17.5 million goal, including funds for the University endowment, new buildings on campus, and increases in salaries to retain key senior members of the faculty.

Shirley Farr, photograph by Norm Porter, n.d. Archival Photographic Files

leadership could be of real service to the University." But there still were those, especially "most of the men who attended the meetings of the Endowment Fund Committee or the Alumni Council," who "had very little idea of the purpose of any educational institution, or of the particular qualities of our own University." To increase the understanding of such donors in the future, the University would have to broaden the range of contributors (including more women) and educate them more effectively about the real needs and purposes of the University.

Shirley Farr (1851-1957) had several strong and mutually reinforcing connections to the University—she was an alumna (Ph.B., 1904), a faculty instructor, and also a member of a prominent Chicago family. Her father, Albert Farr, was a native Vermonter whose lucrative business partnership with Norman Wait Harris, the founder of the Harris Trust and Savings Bank of Chicago, provided Shirley Farr with a comfortable and independent lifestyle. Following her graduation from college, Farr served as an associate professor of history and French at

Shirley Farr

"Giving [to the University] without blowing a trumpet [is] an injustice to the other alumnae of the University," University of Chicago alumna Shirley Farr wrote to Ernest DeWitt Burton in November, 1923. Upset that some men at the University sought to keep women off "important committee[s]," she regarded official silence about her own donations as a missed opportunity to show the community at large the valuable roles that women could and did play in supporting the University: "A good majority of the women and a considerable number of the men," Farr continued, "do know what a university is for, and with proper encouragement and

Honoré de Balzac. *Le secret des Ruggieri*, 1835. MS 437. Gift of Shirley Farr. Codex Manuscript Collection. (detail)

Ripon College, where she later accepted a position on the board of trustees and became a major donor. Returning to the University of Chicago, she held a position as Assistant in History from 1914 to 1917 and a half-time appointment as Instructor in History and departmental counselor from 1929 to 1934.

Shirley Farr's philanthropy was guided by the thematic emphasis on University programs prominently featured in President Burton's campaign. In 1924, she provided a gift of $1,000 annually for five years for the purchase of manuscripts for the Library under the direction of a faculty committee composed of English professor John Matthews Manly, Romance languages scholar William A. Nitze, and medieval historian James Westfall Thompson. By 1929, Farr's manuscript fund, which was established in honor of her father, had purchased twenty-five such manuscripts, including the illuminated fourteenth-century *La jeu de echecs moralises* of Jacques de Cessoles, two beautiful fifteenth-century manuscripts of Boccaccio, *Elegia di Madonna Fiametta* and *Teseida*, and a fourteenth-century manuscript of Guido delle Colonne's *Le livre du gouvernement des rois et des princes*.

Shirley Farr made other gifts reflecting her broad and thoughtful interest in programmatic support for the University. Beginning in 1929, Farr contributed gifts amounting to $14,500 to establish an endowment for the Cleo Hearon Fellowship in History, which was named after a fellow University alumna (Ph.B., 1903; Ph.M., 1909; Ph.D., 1913) and professor of history at Agnes Scott College in Georgia. In the same year, Farr provided the first of many gifts that would total $25,000 in support of the University's general development fund. She made other donations in support of causes as diverse as the William Rainey Harper Memorial Library Fund, the Medical School, the Quadrangle Club, the Institute of Sacred Literature, the School of Social Service Administration, and the Law School, where she contributed to the James Parker Hall Professorship endowment. By 1939, when the Board of Trustees took special note of her cumulative contributions, she had donated more than $62,000 to the University of Chicago.

Shirley Farr's gifts were not only committed to the academic units of the University. She also proved to be a loyal alumna for the University at large, serving as a member of the Board of Alumni Relations and contributing regularly to the alumni gift fund. From the time of her return to the campus just before World War I, she also became involved with the University of Chicago Settlement League, a voluntary association supporting the work of the University of Chicago Settlement in the Back-of-the-Yards neighborhood. In 1923, Shirley Farr provided $3,000 for the purchase of land for what became Camp Farr, the League's fresh-air children's summer camp near Chesterton, Indiana. Later known as Camp Brueckner-Farr, this benefaction was a fitting expression of Farr's lifelong concern for the welfare of the University and the community of which it was a part.

Harold H. Swift, n.d.
Archival Photographic Files

Harold H. Swift and the Swift Family

Few early donors to the University of Chicago gave so consistently and yet so quietly as Harold Swift. An alumnus (Ph.B., 1907) and longtime member and President and Chairman of the Board of Trustees (the latter role from 1922 to 1949), Swift was deeply devoted to "his school," a commitment he demonstrated time and again and often by means of anonymous contributions. His donation of the Swift Prize in Civil Government in 1909 launched what was to become a distinguished career of philanthropy at the University Chicago. Harold Swift was also a family gadfly, mobilizing members of his family on behalf of the University. Swift money, channeled through Harold, subsidized the Library as well as numerous departments, research projects, student prize funds, lectureships, and endowed professorships.

Swift Hall, laying of the cornerstone, 1924. Archival Photographic Files

A life-long bachelor, Harold Swift (1885-1965) seemed so consumed by his work that he failed to develop deep social relationships beyond his family. Rather, he dedicated his life to the University, manifesting, according to historian Dorothy V. Jones, a powerful sense of proprietorship toward the institution. A businessman willingly swallowed up within a community of articulate and opinionated scholars, he occasionally seemed like a fish out of water. But Swift valiantly defended "his" community against its enemies, seen and unseen. When various forces in the 1930s sought to characterize the University of Chicago as a hotbed of radicalism, he responded briskly with countervailing evidence. As Chairman of the Board, he had the responsibility, he believed, to "understand and interpret the institution to the public."

A large share of Swift's personal donations (along with thousands of his books) went to strengthen the Library, though he occasionally directed funds elsewhere. The "best expenditure of funds" for educational purposes, he declared, "is to make the best places better." Thus, he established the William Vaughn Moody Lectures in 1917 with a pledge of $1,500 a year for five years to bring eminent scholars to campus. He also provided part of the funds needed to acquire the Morton Collection of Drama in 1928, a comprehensive collection of published and unpublished play scripts.

One of Swift's most effective contributions was the $5,000 he gave to help poet and editor Harriet Monroe continue the publication of *Poetry* magazine. In return, Monroe agreed to bequeath her personal papers and editorial files to the University (along with the residue of the $5,000 gift). Monroe's *Poetry* manuscript files, received by the Library in 1936, and the funds to continue acquiring contemporary poetry, became the core of the University's impressive holdings in modern poetry and literature. Swift also supported the work of the Department of Music and the University Opera Association, and he gave a large donation in

Carl Sandburg, "The Windy City," early version, typescript, n.d. *Poetry: A Magazine of Verse* Records, 1912-1936. (detail)

1920s to an alumni committee organized to buy manuscripts for the Library. He even gave animals raised on his Michigan summer estate property to the Department of Medicine for scientific research.

Nor was Swift's generosity limited to his own gifts. He also encouraged the members of his family to support the University. The Swifts dominated giving in the 1920s, favoring especially the kinds of programmatic donations that the development campaign of 1924-26 encouraged.

Harold's older brother Charles, along with his mother Ann, contributed heavily to building and research funds. After establishing the Gustavus F. Swift Fellowship in Chemistry in 1908, Ann Swift quickly eclipsed this initial donation with an array of contributions to medical research (a total of $100,000 to match the $200,000 Harold and Charles gave jointly), other research endowments, and the construction of Swift Hall as the new home for the Divinity School (completed in 1926). Charles continued his mother's example by establishing one of President Burton's new endowed professorships, the Charles H. Swift Distinguished Service Professorship, in 1926. He also donated to a variety of other campus causes, including faculty travel grants and departmental research funds. In 1929, with an initial transfer of Swift and Company stock worth $50,500, Charles created the nucleus of a special fund to which he added regular increments of $15,000 or more amounting to a total of $130,000 within the following two years. Dedicated initially to endowing the Distinguished Professorship named in his honor, the Charles H. Swift fund continued to grow with additional gifts in the years that followed and still serves as a major support for undergraduate education.

Harold also encouraged sisters Ruth Swift Maguire and Helen Swift-Neilson to donate to the University. Ruth's discretionary fund bought the University's first cyclotron, funded Arthur Compton's cosmic ray research, established the school's Institute of Statistics, and funded publication of the second volume of the *Dictionary of American English*. She also gave toward the purchase of John M. Manly's personal library and helped the University acquire the Grant Collection of English Bibles in the 1940s.

Swift family, n.d. Archival Photographic Files. Standing from left to right: Ruth, Harold, Gustavus, Jr., Charles. Seated in middle: Gustavus, Sr. and Ann.

The gifts of Helen Swift Neilson and Charles Swift transformed the Library's American literature holdings into nationally renowned collections, especially in the field of drama. In 1917, Percy Boynton in the English Department recognized that "the time was ripe for a more extensive and systematic study of American literature." Boynton set out to establish a program of courses and encourage graduate students to pursue research in this field. To accomplish his goal library resources were needed, and these—readily available at Eastern institutions—were sorely lacking at Chicago. With the support of John Manly and President Judson, Boynton explained the situation to Harold Swift and his sister, Helen Swift-Neilson (then Mrs. Edward Morris). Beginning with an initial gift and continuing by creating an endowed fund, Mrs. Neilson established what was later designated the William Vaughn Moody collection after the prominent author and University faculty member. By the early 1940s the collection numbered approximately 15,000 volumes and included works by famous and obscure authors, many in first and early editions.

In 1925 Charles Swift supported the acquisition of a literature collection formed by F. W. Atkinson of Brooklyn. The collection included several thousand early American plays and was considered stronger in this area than Harvard's, then the most comprehensive. A group of 73 early American novels was purchased from Atkinson with support from Mrs. Neilson in 1931; and during the 1930s, Charles Swift supported the purchase of additional theatrical resources and a large collection of motion picture "stills."

By the time of Harold's death in 1965 he could look back with great pride on his family's extraordinary philanthropy in support of Chicago. Harold Swift was a worthy successor to those heroic early donors, like Rockefeller, Ryerson, and Hutchinson, who had the determination and courage to launch the new University.

Frank R. and Frances Crane Lillie

The charitable work of Frank R. and Frances Crane Lillie was deeply informed by a balance of religious conviction and intellectual commitment. A confirmed rationalist, Frank Lillie took great satisfaction in supporting scientific research at the University of Chicago, while his wife found no greater pleasure than in distributing religious articles and books to friends and acquaintances. Considered separately, they represented opposing poles in their philanthropic values, but together they provided a matchless example of farsighted giving.

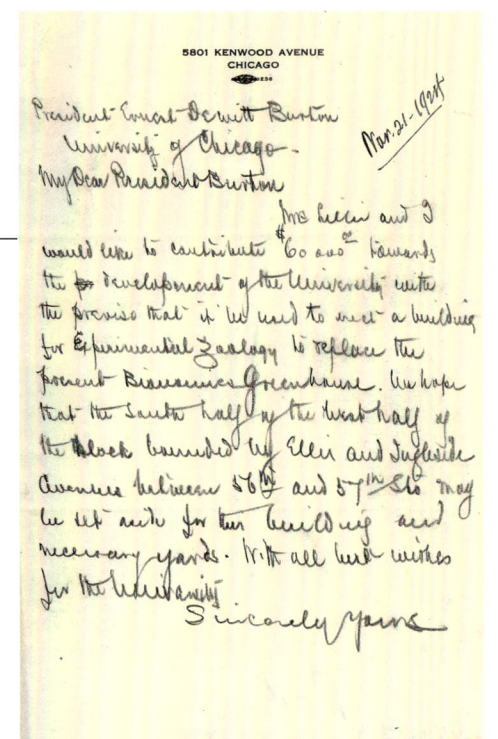

Frances Crane (1869-1958) was the daughter of Richard Teller Crane, a Chicago capitalist and manufacturer who created a huge national business empire built on metal and ceramic products such as lightning rods, railroad equipment, valves, and plumbing fixtures. His great fortune catapulted his family into the city's upper echelons and made his daughter, Frances Crane, a wealthy woman.

Frances Crane Lillie to Ernest D. Burton, unsigned manuscript letter, March 21, 1924. Frank R. Lillie Papers

Frank R. Lillie, n.d. Archival Photographic Files

Whitman Laboratory, under construction, photograph by Chicago Architectural Photographing Company, October 31, 1925. Archival Photographic Files

Frances's political radicalism and her unorthodox religious beliefs, however, embarrassed her father and made her the black sheep of the family. Her participation in the International Ladies' Garment Workers Union strike of 1915 outraged the other Cranes (with the exception of her older brother Charles), as did her adoption of a mystical Catholicism, tinged later in life with elements of Zen Buddhism.

However embarrassing her family found such behavior, it proved attractive to Frank Lillie (1870-1947), a student of Charles O. Whitman, the eminent University of Chicago zoologist and director of the Marine Biology Laboratory at Woods Hole, Massachusetts. In 1896, Frank Lillie and Frances Crane were married. After initial academic appointments at the University of Michigan and Vassar, the Lillies moved to Chicago in 1900 when Frank was offered an assistant professor position in the Department of Zoology. When Whitman died in 1910, his protégé Lillie replaced him as chair of the department, a position that he held until he was appointed the first Dean of the Division of Biological Sciences in 1931.

Frank and Frances Lillie divided their gifts along the fault line of their personal priorities—Frank supported scientific research on campus, while Frances's gifts to the University typically went to the Library. When asked by Library officials if she knew anyone who would buy a collection of books relating to English religious history for the Library, Mrs. Lillie gladly donated the necessary funds. Continuing an interest begun during the Harper administration, her older brother Charles Crane also made numerous contributions to the University, with the bulk of his donations designated for programs in Russian and Slavic studies.

As Chairman of the Department of Zoology, Frank R. Lillie was responsible for the couple's most conspicuous donation to the University of Chicago, the construction of the Whitman Laboratory of Experimental Biology. According to a budgetary analysis done in 1925, the Lillies' initial donation of $60,000 in 1924 was insufficient to meet the full costs. Undeterred, the couple added more than $30,000 to their pledge, $4,000 of which went toward equipping the building. To this very substantial gift, the Lillies then added others. Beginning in 1907, they contributed funds for research trips and projects of faculty colleagues. Their final gift to the University, presented by Mrs. Lillie in 1938, was Crane and Company stock worth $10,000 to be used as the basis of an endowment in support of a cooperative nursery on campus.

I have learned that a donor is one who receives, not one who gives. This clinic will not only assist in giving students sound bodies and sound minds, but it will be of great service to the people of Chicago. By serving the city well, the University will be brought closer to the hearts of the people of Chicago.

Max Epstein
The University Record, New Series, vol. 14, no. 1 (January 1928)

Culmination of an Era

Developing the Medical Center

Thanks to the spirit of Ernest Burton's bold development campaign, the University's hospitals and clinics enjoyed ample funding after 1925. Given the importance of creating a nationally significant medical center and hospital complex in Chicago, donors and University officials emphasized the cause of medical research and quality health care. Such attention paid off, and by the late 1920s the first stages of the University's massive medical building program were reaching completion.

The achievements of the later 1920s grew from the promising accomplishments of the preceding decade, most notably the commitment of the family of Albert Merritt Billings in 1916 to erect a large hospital building on the University campus. Albert Billings' son, C. K. G. Billings, was the family's principal donor, but his cousin Dr. Frank Billings (the Dean of Rush Medical College), brother-in-law Charles H. Ruddock, and nephew Albert M. B. Ruddock also participated in the plan. In all, members of the Billings family gave more than $1 million to found the University of Chicago Medical School and erect the Albert M. Billings Hospital. Yet, even with this substantial support, the University was not able to open Billings Hospital until 1927, due to the war and higher post-war construction costs.

The momentum created by the development campaign of 1924-26 energized other major donors to support the hospitals. Colonel and Mrs. John Roberts matched the Billings family's million-dollar donation and enabled the University to break ground for the Bobs Roberts Memorial Hospital for Children in 1927. John Roberts was a native of County Clare, Ireland, who had come to Chicago and made his fortune as the president, treasurer, and general manager of Roberts & Oake, a meat packing firm headquartered at Chicago's Union Stock Yards. Deeply saddened in 1917 by the death of their five-year-old son Charles Radnor, affectionately nicknamed Bobs, the Robertses pledged $1 million dollars to the University of Chicago for a new pediatric hospital. Their gift was enhanced by two contributions from the Rockefeller-funded General Education Board, one of $175,000 for the construction of the research laboratories of Bobs Roberts Hospital, and the other of $1 million as an endowment to support research and teaching in the Department of Pediatrics.

Affiliation agreements between city hospitals and the University also brought forth new donors. Contributions establishing the Elizabeth Spalding McElwee Memorial and Gertrude Dunn Hicks Memorial made possible two new hospital facilities in 1931, each offering a fifty-bed clinic operating under the auspices of the Chicago Home for Destitute and Crippled Children at 59th Street and Ellis Avenue. In addition, Dr. Joseph B. DeLee, the founder of Chicago Lying-In Hospital, together with Janet Ayer Fairbank of the Women's Board and the Mother's Aid Club, raised $1 million to erect a new hospital building. On April 29, 1931, a new, state-of-the-art facility for the Chicago Lying-In Hospital opened its doors at 58th Street and Maryland Avenue and assumed its place as a central element in the University's expanding medical complex.

The decision to move Chicago Lying-In Hospital to the campus of the University was due largely to the efforts of Joseph Bolivar DeLee. Dr. DeLee was a late-nineteenth century pioneer who devoted his life to providing socially responsible medical care to the women of Chicago. Trained at the Chicago Medical School, DeLee received his M.D. in 1891. Rather than devote himself to a

Dr. Joseph B. DeLee, ca. 1940.
Archival Photographic Files

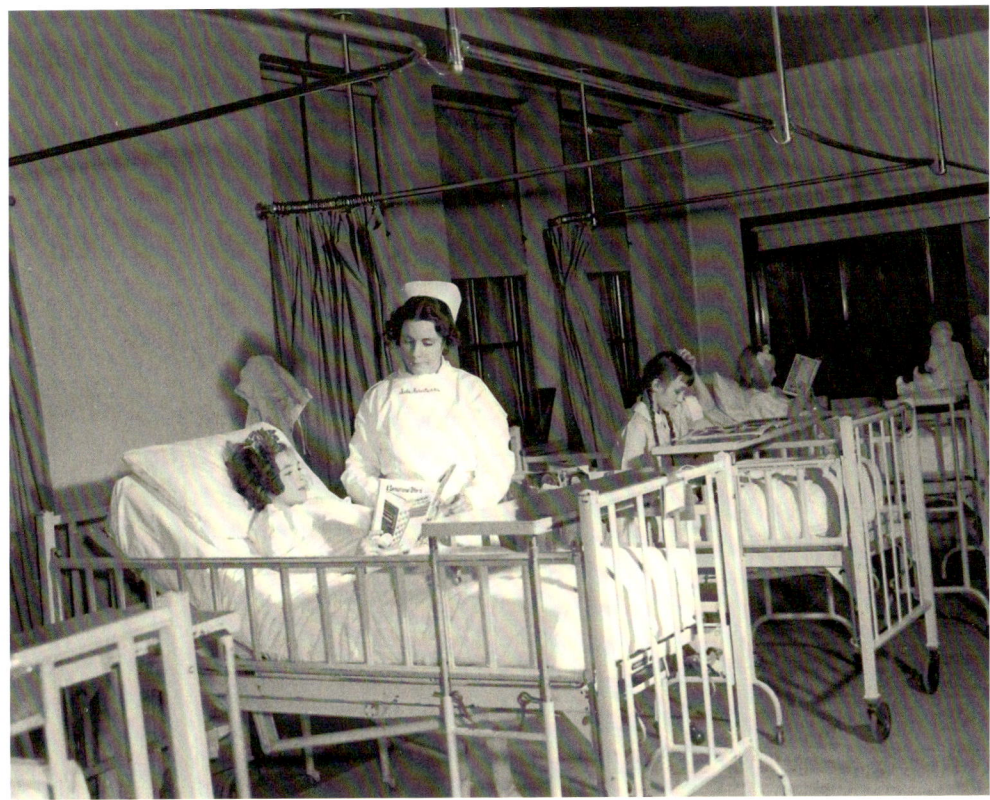

Bobs Roberts Hospital Ward, n.d.
Archival Photographic Files

Gertrude D. Hicks, n.d.
Archival Photographic Files

lucrative private practice, DeLee decided in 1896 to establish a clinic to provide decent obstetrical care to poor pregnant women residing in the slums. Renting rooms on Maxwell Street on the city's West Side, he provided care for over 200 women (most of whom were poor or recent immigrants or both) and trained sixty-four students and physicians in practical obstetrics. Initial success on Maxwell Street gave DeLee the opportunity to transfer his practice in 1899 to a remodeled home on Ashland Avenue, where he increased his clinic's capacity to thirteen beds. This new venue remained a shoestring operation—after paying his first month's rent and purchasing necessary equipment, DeLee had sixty-one cents left to his name. DeLee's heroic commitment to his cause slowly gained the support of local Chicago patrons, however, and in 1914 he opened what was now officially named the Lying-In Hospital on a site at 51st Street and Vincennes Avenue (where Provident Hospital now stands). Here, the vast impact of his clinics immediately became clear—operating three free dispensaries, by 1927 DeLee and his associates had treated over 69,000 mothers and their babies, as well as 20,000 gynecological patients. In the same thirteen-year period, his hospital delivered 28,735 babies and cared for over 10,000 obstetrical and gynecological cases. In gaining affiliation with the University of Chicago in 1927 and making its final move to the campus of the University in 1930, Chicago Lying-In Hospital was now assured a distinguished and secure future.

Institutional Donors

Not all gifts of substance to the University of Chicago came from individual donors. Institutional donors and foundations had supported the work of the new University from its very inception. In 1889-90 the American Baptist Education Society acted as the conduit through which John D. Rockefeller made his initial contributions to the University.

Although John D. Rockefeller's Final Gift to the University occurred in December, 1910, the various charitable foundations he established helped to sustain the Rockefeller family's relationship with Chicago into the 1930s. The first of these foundations, the General Education Board (GEB), was created in 1903 to support improvements in education for African-American communities in the South. Under the terms of its federal charter the GEB expanded its orbit to "the promotion of education within the United States without distinction of race, sex, or creed," guaranteeing that the Board would support private research institutions like the University of Chicago. The Board began funding medical education at the University in 1916, and it enlarged its philanthropic impact in 1925, when it gave two substantial gifts to the University totaling over $1 million each for

The Research Laboratory of the Institute of American Meat Packers, Founded by Thomas E. Wilson at The University of Chicago, printed pamphlet, ca. 1936. University Presidents' Papers, 1925-1945

> The Research Laboratory
> of the
> Institute of American
> Meat Packers
> Founded by Thomas E. Wilson
> at The University of Chicago
>
> ———
>
> *A Co-operative Endeavor
> Between
> the University and the Institute*

research in the sciences and humanities.

Other Rockefeller-funded foundations supported medical education, social work, and research in the social sciences. The Rockefeller Foundation, which was created in 1909 and chartered in 1913, began its charitable work by campaigning to cure hookworm in the American South and overseas. The Foundation moved on to support research on malaria and yellow fever, and it funded the establishment of the Peking Union Medical College in China. With support from Rockefeller Foundation grants totaling more than $2.75 million by 1930, the University of Chicago was able to launch its Medical School, develop its first Department of Psychiatry, strengthen advanced pro-

Trustees of the General Education Board at the Hotel Samoset, Rockland, Maine, July, 1915. Front row, second from left: Frederick T. Gates; fourth from left: Harry Pratt Judson. Second row, third from left: John D. Rockefeller, Jr. Reproduction from Frederick T. Gates, *Chapters in My Life*, New York: Free Press, 1977

grams in the humanities, and expand professional training in the School of Social Service Administration. Another Rockefeller philanthropy, the Laura Spelman Rockefeller Memorial, provided essential support for the University's Local Community Research Committee and Social Science Research Committee and funded the erection of the Social Science Research Building in 1929; the Memorial's grants amounted to more than $3 million by the end of the decade.

A series of grants from other sources in the 1920s created important programs in medical research and expanded the range of the University's work. In 1921, the Otho S. A. Sprague Memorial Institute entered into a special affiliation with the University of Chicago; for twenty-three years, until reverting to its status as an independent corporation in 1944, all of the income from its endowment was committed exclusively to medical research at the University. The Lasker Foundation for Medical Research, established in 1928 by a gift of $1 million to the University of Chicago from Albert D. and Flora W. Lasker, devoted all of its income to research on degenerative diseases conducted at the University; after 1939, at the decision of Mr. Lasker, the scope of its support for medical research was broadened to include investigations of other diseases.

Scientific research of a different kind was initiated by the Institute of American Meat Packers, the Chicago-based trade and research association of more than 300 American meat packing companies. In 1923, under the auspices of the Institute, Arthur Lowenstein, vice-president of Chicago meat packer Wilson & Company, provided $7,500 over three years for a

Max Epstein Dispensary, n.d.
Archival Photographic Files

fellowship at the University of Chicago supporting research on scientific problems related to the meat packing industry. This gift was followed the next year by a gift from meat-packing executive Thomas E. Wilson of $15,000 over three years to establish a research laboratory of the Institute of American Meat Packers on the University of Chicago campus. Opened in 1925 in a newly erected building at 939 East 57th Street under a cooperative agreement with the University, the Institute's research laboratory investigated problems such as the chemistry of sterilizing agents, stabilization of pigmentation, and improved chemical processes for curing.

Scientists in University laboratories were not alone in benefiting from the largesse of the new private foundations and institutional donors. In May 1926, Frederick P. Keppel, president of the Carnegie Corporation, informed University President Max Mason that his foundation was committing $1,385,000 for the establishment of a graduate library school at the University of Chicago. The Carnegie grant was designed to take advantage of the University's rich interdisciplinary research tradition and provide students considering library careers "the opportunity for the broadest possible professional education." The Carnegie grant assured the formation of the nation's first graduate library institution, the Graduate Library School, and launched the University's distinguished contributions to the development of library and information studies.

Max Epstein

Max Epstein (1875-1954) was a farsighted businessman and philanthropist whose most generous pledge was made just as the international business collapse of 1929 dramatically constricted nearly all giving to institutions. Born in Cincinnati, Epstein briefly attended City College in New York before moving to Chicago in 1891. Thereafter, he set out to make a considerable fortune. A leading local industrialist—he was the chairman of the General American Tank Car Company—Epstein was also a member of the Board of Trustees of the Art Institute of Chicago from 1930 to 1953. A lifelong collector of Old Masters, Epstein's bequest of twenty-five early European paintings in 1954 was a notable addition to the Art Institute's collections. Max Epstein's connections to the University began in 1917, when he gave the first of a series of gifts to the hospitals. The Max Epstein Clinic at 59th Street and Maryland Avenue was incorporated as a wing of the Chicago Lying-In Hospital.

In many ways Max Epstein stood at the end of the classic era of private philanthropy at the University of Chicago, for his most significant gift—an unrealized institute of the fine arts—was conceived in the context of the goals of President Burton's campaign of 1924-26. Under Burton's successor, Max Mason, the University was able to secure major gifts from George H. Jones in 1926 to build a second chemistry building, from Bernard A. Eckhart in 1927 for a mathematics building, from Albert D. Lasker in 1928 for the Medical School, and from Bernard E. Sunny in 1928 for the Laboratory School's gymnasium, all of which seemed to confirm hopes for additional major donations. The stock market crash of 1929 swept away these expectations, and the harsh economic environment of the 1930s made Burton's lofty goals seem sadly illusory. The fate of Max Epstein's gift was an early sign of the grave financial and fundraising challenges that lay ahead.

Proposed Institute of Fine Arts,
Paul Phillippe Cret, architect,
architectural drawing, n.d.
Architectural Drawings Collection

Max Epstein was inspired by Ernest Burton's suggestion that the University needed a first-rate center for research and teaching in the fine arts. In *The University of Chicago in 1940*, Burton had argued "[i]t is to be hoped that long before the year 1940 comes around, the University will have erected at least one beautiful building devoted wholly to the fine arts, and established in it skilled interpreters of these arts to the University community." Burton's dream seemed closer to reality when the University secured a million-dollar pledge from Epstein to support the creation of an Institute of Fine Arts, to be housed in a building with classrooms and galleries located adjacent to a planned undergraduate residential quadrangle on 60th Street between Kimbark and Woodlawn.

In his letter of gift for the art building, Max Epstein wrote, "I believe that the University of Chicago should offer to the young men and women who are its students and to the public at large the opportunity of learning the significance of Art, both as a history of the life of the past and as a living and inspiring force in the present. The creation of an art center at the University will bring together a body of teachers and students of Art and will result in the spreading of a sincere and informed appreciation of Art."

Unfortunately, Epstein made his pledge on August 30, 1929, only a few weeks before the Great Crash. The University initiated a planning effort for the new building, even obtaining preliminary drawings by the noted architect of Beaux-Arts classicism, Paul P. Cret. But in January 1931, when the preliminary design process was completed, Epstein's initial gift of $15,000 for the art building was shifted, with his consent, to the Hospitals, and the University decided not to pursue the construction of the Institute of Fine Arts. President Robert Hutchins laconically and somewhat ambiguously reported to the Board of Trustees in 1935 that "[i]n 1929 we had hopes of the Art Department, for a new chairman was found for it and a donor pledged a million dollars to provide quarters for it. On account of the Depression neither the chairman nor the donor has been able to realize his ambitions for the Department." Other generous University donors were also disappointed by these frustrated hopes. In 1929 and 1930, Mrs. Frances Crane Lillie had given the University two ornamental doors by artist Alfeo Faggi, the Dante Door and the Door of St. Francis, with the intention that they be mounted in the entrance to a University art museum. But with the dwindling of the University's ambitions for an art building, the doors were returned to the donor in 1939.

In the end, an Institute of Fine Arts was never built, and with the exception of a few buildings finished in 1931 and 1932 such as International House and the Field House, construction on the campus of the University of Chicago ceased for more than a decade. And three decades would pass before the next fundraising campaign, when generous and civic-minded donors, strong presidential leadership, and a strong economic climate coalesced to create a powerful new vision for the educational future of the University of Chicago.

Max Epstein, n.d.
Archival Photographic Files